Prai

Enginᴇᴇ⊏ıı ıɥ
the **DIGITAL**
Transformation

MW00576146

It's hard to believe that we've had to wait this long for a book about how to scale digital transformations. *Engineering the Digital Transformation* provides a step-by-step guide for businesses that want to drive continuous improvement successfully across their software organizations. Gary's knowledge and expertise in both manufacturing and software make him the perfect guide, and this easy to read, accessible, and smart book belongs on the bookshelves of every CTO and CIO in the industry.

—**Basheer Janjua**
CTO Forum President

Once again Gary has illustrated for us that the keys to developing great software and existing products are hiding in plain sight. Exploring the ideas from thinkers like Deming, Goldratt, and countless others – through the filter of his own hard won experiences leading DevOps transformations for decades, Gary has written an easy-to-read, thoughtful and thorough book that we all can learn from.

—**Rick Cochran**
CTO, Experity

Gary has a sophisticated level of experience and understanding of the modern Digital Transformation. He provided our team with proven techniques to get us started, deep insights along the way and served as a rich sounding board for our ideas that enabled us to proceed with confidence on our Journey to bi-weekly releases.

—**Ted Youel**
Senior Principle Engineer,
Optum Technology

Engineering the Digital Transformation is exactly the book the software industry needs as we work to improve outcomes and quality. It challenges the software industry to learn the hard won lessons from our siblings in manufacturing; control inventory, reduce operational cost, and improve throughput. It also translates our industry in understandable ways to our business partners who depend on, but do not understand, the the flexibility and complexity inherent in software. Gary's background in both manufacturing and software delivery is telling and the ideas he raises for helping leadership monitor progress are exciting. There is great value here.

—**Bryan Finster**
Delivery System Engineer,
Walmart Labs

Software engineering organizations too often do not deliver products in a predictable fashion with a high level of initial quality. *Engineering the Digital Transformation* provides an actionable framework to successfully deliver on the expectations of digital transformation in a repeatable, scalable manner.

—**Kent Eckert**
Vice President Retail Technology,
Save-a-lot

Engineering

the **DIGITAL**

Transformation

Engineering
the DIGITAL
Transformation

GARY GRUVER

Foreword by JIM HIGHSMITH

Copyright © 2019 by Gary Gruver
All rights reserved, for information about permission to reproduce
selections from this book, write to gary@garygruver.com

Cover and book design by Devon Smith
Author photograph by Carolyn Gruver

ISBN: 978-1-54397-526-0
eBook ISBN: 978-1-54397-548-2

Publisher's note to readers: Many of the ideas, quotations, and paraphrases
attributed to different thinkers and industry leaders herein are excerpted
from informal conversations, correspondence, interviews, conference
round-tables, and other forms of oral communication that took place over
the development and writing of this book. Although the author(s)
and publisher have made every effort to ensure that the information in
this book was correct at press time, the author and publisher do not
assume and hereby disclaim any liability to any party for any loss, damage,
or disruption caused by errors or omissions, whether such errors or
omissions result from negligence, accident, or any other cause.

For information about special discounts for bulk purchases
or for information on booking Gary Gruver for an event,
please visit www.garygruver.com.

ENGINEERING THE DIGITAL TRANSFORMATION

Contents

Foreword

Do the names Ohno, Goldratt, Deming, or Taylor resonate with you? Do the practices of Kata, time-in-motion studies, Just-in-Time, Drum Buffer Rope, Kanban (do you know its origin?), or Theory of Constraints ring a bell? These are people and practices that have driven continuous improvement in manufacturing. Are these also applicable to software development? Gary thinks so and he has developed a framework for helping companies with their agile continuous improvement initiatives by adopting and adapting these manufacturing practices for software deployment to help you compete in the critical digital world of the future.

I met Gary over a decade ago when he was a Director of engineering at HP working on replacing technical debt ridden legacy software for each LaserJet printer with integrated software that operated across the entire product line. The huge success of this product development effort was the topic of his first book, *A Practical Approach to Large-Scale Agile Development: How HP Transformed LaserJet FutureSmart Firmware*. I was intrigued by his success and how his approach differed from most agile transitions. Gary brought his years of hardware engineering experience to bear on the issue of improving software development products and processes.

This book *Engineering the Digital Transformation* builds on his earlier work, several years of applying these practices while a VP at Macy's, and recent years of consulting with a wide range of clients.

There are two fundamental ideas in this book. First is the application of proven manufacturing continuous improvement concepts to software development. Not only does Gary review these concepts, but he also describes how they can be modified to fit software development. The second important idea is to separate the concepts of product development from product deployment. Development covers all the front-end processes (or as Gary says, the left-side processes) while Deployment covers the back-end ones such as building, testing, and configuring. Development is a manual creative process while deployment is a prescriptive, automated (hopefully) one. Furthermore, in hardware development these two processes are typically serial, while for software development, because software is malleable, they should operate in parallel. A problem that Gary points out is that many traditional software development organizations still operate as if development and deployment are serial in nature—a holdover from the waterfall development era. Organizations that don't see the concurrent nature of these two concepts fail to utilize the unique differences between hardware and software to their advantage. Converting development practices from waterfall to agile is only half the transformation job—you need the kind of deployment process Gary describes in this book.

The advantage of separating development from deployment concepts is that you can apply appropriate practices to each. For example, the software development community has picked up the term "repeatable" from manufacturing process control. But development practices are not repeatable in that sense because the inputs are so variable and humans, not machines, execute the processes. But the development process can be "reliable" as teams figure out how to deliver customer value by learning and adapting as they go. When automated, the deployment process can be repeatable, maybe not to the extent of manufacturing processes, but close enough. Gary uses the term stable quality signal to indicate progress in bringing the deployment process under control. An un-stable quality signal indicates unacceptable variation in the process and the measurement components suggest where to attack the variability so they do become repeatable.

Some in the agile community have abandoned the word engineering for something creative sounding like crafting. Looking at Gary's work you can see that both are correct—if applied appropriately to development and deployment. The tasks of defining goals, determining value outcome measures, identifying features and stories, writing good tests, creating evolutionary architectures, and more certainly fall into the crafting realm. Likewise, automating tests (another example, coding is a creative activity while managing that code is an engineering one), building, running tests, and creating deployment pipelines are engineering activities.

Finally, you can't introduce new concepts and expect people to adapt by continuing to use the same performance measures that got you in trouble in the first place. For example, in project management I introduced the agile triangle (value, quality, constraints) as a replacement for the traditional iron triangle (scope, schedule, cost). Gary suggests replacing "commitment to plan" with "optimizing flow." If you have a good prioritized backlog of features to be implemented, then the best way to get the highest throughput is to optimize the flow through the entire development pipeline. Using measurements to establish a stable quality signal, deployment processes can be automated and tweaked to maximize the flow of customer value. Of course, managing flow is easier if you re-organize around products (or business capabilities) rather than projects as Gary suggests.

I frequently wonder why "agile" concepts and practices have continued to be relevant for more than twenty years. Most "fads" tend to come, and then go. I think we can safely say that agile is no longer a fad, but a sustainable movement. Why? I think there are two reasons: One, agile persists because it is built on a conceptual foundation, the Agile Manifesto, that people related to on many levels. Second, "agile" has become a container for innovation and growth. Kanban, DevOps and many other concepts and practices have been incorporated into organization's agile transformations. Gary's *Engineering the Digital Transformation*, brings yet another innovation to extend the agile movement even further.

Jim Highsmith
Original signatory of the Agile Manifesto
Lafayette, Colorado
June 2019

Introduction

The world is transitioning from a capital-based economy with manufacturing as a key component toward a knowledge-based economy that is much more dependent on software. The manufacturing-based economy is fairly mature, and engineering practices have evolved to be very efficient and effective at improving manufacturing. This is the result of a lot of great people building on each other's contributions over the years to provide systematic approaches to improvement.

Readers with a software background may not be aware of what manufacturing leaders have achieved. Therefore, we will highlight a few key leaders and the impact of their approaches. W. Edwards Deming went to Japan after WWII and helped the country evolve from one known for low-cost and low-quality products to a leading economy known for their outstanding quality. Taiichi Ohno created a culture and approach to continuous improvement that is credited for making Toyota the most dominant manufacturer of automobiles in the world with average net profit sales over 70% higher than industry avarage between 2003 and 2008 (Goldratt 2006)." Eliyahu Goldratt introduced the "Theory of Constraints" approach that enabled organizations across many different industries to dramatically improve productivity with manufacturing organizations seeing 70% improvement in throughput on average (Goldratt, 2005, chap. 2).

The software industry, on the other hand, is fairly new and has not developed the same systematic approaches to improvements. In fact, the motivation for this book grew out of the frustration I felt watching consulting business clients struggle to achieve the results I knew were possible as quickly as I would have liked. I started my career as a process engineer in manufacturing and was very focused on learning from the thought leaders to help me drive improvements. When I started working in software a couple of decades ago, I was still focused on continuous improvement, but I began to realize that software was a different beast. I learned as much as I could from leading large software transformations and by reading what others were saying in the industry. There were a lot of great ideas out there, but they were more focused on applying the latest and greatest practices and seemed to lack the systematic engineering rigor I had learned as a process engineer in manufacturing.

I came to the conclusion that if software development was going to improve faster we needed more engineering rigor and systematic approaches for prioritizing improvements and quantifying the impact of changes. When faced with this challenge the natural reaction of most people is to learn how we leverage the approaches that worked well for manufacturing and apply them directly to software. In fact, as I go to software conferences now, I hear more and more that the software industry is just learning to do what the manufacturing industry learned years ago. As we found out when trying to use waterfall development for software, though, this does not take into account the unique characteristics and capabilities of software. What we need to do instead is first look at what was done in manufacturing and why it was done from a product development and process improvement perspective. Next, we need to really take the time to understand the unique characteristics and capabilities of software. Finally, we need to develop the engineering rigor that can leverage what we have learned from optimizing manufacturing over decades and start developing the engineering approaches that are most appropriate for software.

The goal of this book is to lay the framework for systematic approaches to improving how software is developed for a broad range of applications. Unlike most books in the industry, which concentrate on providing a variety of different practices that have proven to work well for software, this book will focus on high-level principles. These principles are based on what has been proven to work very well in manufacturing, but they will be modified to address software's unique characteristics and capabilities.

Chapter 1 will provide a very simplified review of the evolution in approaches to improvement in manufacturing. It is not intended to be an exhaustive review but, rather, a brief overview of the major approaches, showing what was done and why. The purpose here is to provide a foundation that can be used to leverage the existing approaches to software. It is important to understand these approaches because they have been successfully used and fine-tuned over decades to deliver dramatic results. They are based on high-level principles that can be applied to a broad range of applications and codified in systematic approaches in order to be taught to practitioners. Software needs similar systematic approaches to developing the productivity improvements required to compete in a knowledge-based society, and manufacturing principles need to be modified to work for software. The goal of Chapter 1 is to help the reader understand what systematic approaches are used in manufacturing and why those specific techniques have been successful. Then, instead of just trying to replicate their approaches, we need to understand both what made them successful and why, so that we are in a better position to understand how to modify the approaches for software.

Chapter 2 will provide a brief history of the unique approaches developed for software. Again, it is not intended to be exhaustive but rather to show how and why the software industry is starting to adapt to address its unique characteristics and capabilities. Agile and other approaches were created because practitioners understood that traditional approaches didn't work well for software. It is important to understand the history of these improvements and why they were created as a foundation for pursuing more systematic approaches to software.

Software is very different from manufacturing in a lot of ways, and if we don't take that into consideration, the systematic approaches will not be as effective. These differences need to be understood and appreciated before we start developing systematic approaches for software. Chapter 3 will review the unique characteristics and capabilities of software, including some recent breakthroughs that are enabling different approaches. I will review these differences in detail to lay the foundation for subsequent chapters, where we will review how software needs to modify the different parts of the manufacturing approach to be successful.

The biggest difference between software and manufacturing is that with software we are managing digital rather than physical assets. This has broad implications. For software the deployment pipeline of build, deploy, and test doesn't require the creation of a capital intensive manufacturing process, so the product can be built up from the very first line of code. Additionally, because it is digital once the product is created, it can be used as many times as required, quickly and efficiently, and without having to worry about finished goods inventory and distribution. The combination of not having to worry about finished goods inventory and being able to quickly modify the product being built provides a level of flexibility not possible for physical assets. These advantages have become much more pronounced with two fairly recent changes. The first change is the virtualization of hardware that enables a further separation of digital and physical assets for large software products. The second change is the more recent automation of most of the repetitive build, deploy, and test processes. This dramatically improves the efficiencies of releasing changes to software, enabling it to be even more flexible. Being digital also creates some additional challenges, such as making it harder to see the flow of work through the organization and how the product is coming together. Unlike traditional manufacturing, we can't see inventory flowing through a physical manufacturing line or immediately recognize a quality problem because components don't fit together.

The next five chapters will go into developing and detailing a systematic approach for software. Chapter 4 will focus on approaches to improving product design and development. Chapter 5 will evaluate improving quality. Chapter 6 will look at how to improve the flow through the organization. Chapter 7 will look broadly at approaches for continuous improvement. And Chapter 8 will look at how to modify the software planning process to take advantage of its flexibility. Each chapter will look closely at the different aspects of improvement and what was done in manufacturing, and why, in more detail. Then, it will review the unique characteristics and capabilities of software that apply those processes. And finally, we will review how we should approach improving the way we manage software.

In Chapter 9, we will pull all of these concepts together and provide a framework for a more systematic approach that organizations can use to improve how they manage software. The goal of this book is not to provide all the answers for how to engineer the digital transformation. It is to get people understanding that there can and should be a different approach to engineering software. The hope is that this will get the creative minds in software working with the best minds in process engineering to develop and optimize approaches for the unique characteristics and capabilities of software.

CHAPTER 1

Manufacturing History

From its inception, manufacturing has had a long history of improving both how it develops and how it manufactures products that started off with very manual approaches passed down between generations. The focus on systematic approaches for improving manufacturing is a good place to start. We'll review the major innovators and the improvements they championed and then we'll review the systematic approaches used for product development in manufacturing.

Process Improvements in Manufacturing

The Journeyman and Apprentice Approach

The way the people in manufacturing learned how to build things typically started with a journeyman who had been trained in the techniques. The journeyman would pass this knowledge down to an apprentice, a member of the next generation. The journeyman trained the apprentice by doing the work while the apprentice watched. Over time, the apprentice would start doing the work with feedback from the journeyman. The best practices were passed from one generation to the next, and as the apprentice became more and more experienced and progressed to journeyman status, he could take everything that he had learned and add new and unique approaches to it that hadn't yet been considered. In this way, manufacturing grew more efficient and effective at building better products over time. This approach worked for an extended period during which manufacturing was primarily manual.

Interchangeable Parts

In the 1800s, Eli Whitney began a major shift in US manufacturing with his use of interchangeable parts (Hognose 2014). He was trying to figure out how to help the United States fight wars without enough skilled workers to manufacture the guns required. Using a common design of interchangeable parts enabled him to better leverage a less skilled workforce. They didn't need to go through the journeyman approach and custom make everything. They could figure out how to efficiently and effectively build all the individual parts and then assemble a final product. This was a big breakthrough that enabled a young, inexperienced workforce in the United States to take on more mature countries and win some early battles.

The Assembly Line

Interchangeable parts enabled some fundamentally different approaches in manufacturing and spurred the creation of the assembly factory. The best-known early example is Henry Ford's Model T factory, where he created an efficient, continuous flow through a manufacturing line that began with raw iron ore and resulted in a final product in 81 hours (Goldratt 2006). This efficient process meant that it wasn't necessary for a journeyman to know how to do everything from end to end. Instead, very complex things were broken down into simpler components that could be maximized and quickly assembled. Henry Ford's assembly line created flow through the system by minimizing inventory. He accomplished this by constraining the available space on the assembly line. There just wasn't any room for storing defects to be fixed later. Additionally, problems became visible because the flow in the factory would stop. Things had to be done right the first time, and any issues interrupting the flow were very visible and needed immediate attention. This assembly line with limited space for inventory was a significant breakthrough that made automobiles affordable for the masses. It was based on a very stable, high-volume application for manufacturing.

Time in Motion Studies

The next major innovator to come on the scene was Frederick Winslow Taylor. He was probably the first industrial engineer, and his stopwatch time study, along with Frank Gilbreth's motion studies, eventually resulted in the time and motion study approach (Wikapedia 2019, "Fredrick Winslow Taylor"). This was the beginning of a structured approach to continuous improvement. During his studies, Taylor would watch people work, time the steps that were most efficient, and then work to ensure that all the labors were following the most efficient process. This resulted in some significant improvements in productivity. He faced challenges, though, because he viewed factory workers as a tool to be controlled rather than individuals who could have ideas that would help the process improve. So, while he was really effective in improving productivity, his reputation was damaged because he didn't do a very good job engaging people in the process or getting them to take ownership for the improvements they were required to implement.

Process Control

Over time, automation and consistency in manufacturing increased. Instead of individuals handcrafting products, the process and automation were creating the products. This led to a focus on process engineering to improve quality. W. Edwards Deming is one of the fathers of this quality movement. He figured out that the best way to ensure that we're creating good high-quality products in manufacturing is to consistently monitor the process to make sure that it's always in control (Deming, 1982, chap. 11). This enabled a huge amount of efficiencies because when you aren't building up a lot of poor-quality product that needs to be reworked, you have a more efficient flow of product through the factory. If you build in high quality from the beginning by controlling the process, you have much higher quality and more efficient manufacturing in the end. Deming took these concepts to Japan after World War II. While Japan was once known as a country that produced low-cost, low-quality products, implementation of these processes enabled the country to become a world leader in quality and efficiencies in manufacturing and allowed them to begin dominating the world of manufacturing.

Just-in-Time Inventory

The approach to controlling the process enabled dramatic improvements in quality, but it wasn't enough because it is impossible to always monitor the process well enough to know that you aren't creating a quality problem and a large amount of inventory that needs to be reworked. Taiichi Ohno realized this at Toyota and created the "just-in-time inventory" approach to minimize the risk. This approach focuses on minimizing the amount of inventory in the system that hasn't been assembled into the final product (Poppendieck and Poppendieck 2003, chap. 1). This is important because any inventory that hasn't been assembled is at risk of rework due to the fact that quality problems may not be discovered before inventory is put into the final assembly. Henry Ford had mitigated this problem for a stable, high-volume factory building a single product by constraining space, but Ford's approach did not work as well for applications building a variety of products that couldn't use a linked assembly line.

Cost Accounting

Factories that build a variety of things using common resources need a systematic approach for improving. The cost accounting approach of allocating all the equipment and labor cost to a product enables you to know what it costs to create the product. Using the product cost, your profit is equal to the amount you can sell the product for minus the cost to assemble it. To increase your profit, you either need to increase the selling price or reduce the manufacturing costs. Therefore, the focus on reducing costs is on fully utilizing your people and equipment so their costs can be allocated over more products. This cost accounting approach provides a very systematic way for improving manufacturing that has been widely adopted but is not optimal. It turns out that when you are focused on keeping everyone in the factory busy, they end up building stuff that is not required, and inventory starts stacking up, creating higher capital costs and exposure to rework.

Drum Buffer Rope

Eliyahu Goldratt was the first to point out the flaws in the "keeping everyone busy" approach and took a much more system-wide view of the issue (Goldratt and Cox 2004). He argued that the number of people and equipment in the factory was really a fixed cost, and the way to systematically improve product cost was to focus on improving the flow through the entire factory instead of at each person and piece of equipment. Additionally, he noted that every process does not control flow through the whole factory. Instead, typically there is one bottleneck in the factory that is limiting the flow. This led to his Theory of Constraints systematic approach to improving manufacturing, which is very different and much more effective than cost accounting.

Goldratt's approach to limiting inventory in the system for factories building a variety of products was also very different from Henry Ford's practice of limiting space, because it had to be. Goldratt had factories with lots of different steps that were not connected in an assembly line, and he had to make sure excess inventory was not building up in the system. He accomplished this using his Drum Buffer Rope approach. In this approach, you find the bottleneck in the process and use its cycle time as the fastest cadence the factory can operate at without building up excess inventory. This is the drum that defines the rate of flow. Next, you build a small buffer of inventory in front of the bottleneck to ensure it is never starved of work. Finally, instead of just releasing work into the factory when resources are idle as is done with cost accounting, work is released into the system based on a pull from the bottleneck when it processes inventory (the rope). This approach has enabled a lot of different types of manufacturing organizations to dramatically reduce inventories and improve the flow of products.

Kanban

Taiichi Ohno needed an approach for managing the flow in Toyota's manufacturing lines because he was trying to compete with the US automobile industry, which had high-volume, dedicated factories while Toyota had low-volume factories building a variety of products. Ohno created the Kanban process for managing the flow between each of the individual manufacturing steps. In Kanban, a card or cart is used to signal when the upstream step can start building. Think of this as a tub that holds a limited amount of finished product between each step in the manufacturing process. The upstream process can only create product when the tub comes back from the downstream step after the inventory has been processed. This signals to the upstream process that it can build more product without creating excess inventory. This happens between each manufacturing step so that inventory is minimized throughout, but nothing is starved by moving bottlenecks. This is very different from Drum Buffer Rope, which releases work into the front of the manufacturing process based on a pull from the bottleneck.

Kanban works to ensure that there aren't short-lived bottlenecks being created somewhere else in the system as products ebb and flow through the factory. Ohno optimized the system to a level above Drum Buffer Rope to achieve the efficiencies of Henry Ford's high-volume, stable manufacturing in a low-volume factory with lots of variability.

Toyota Kata

Kanban helped control inventory levels and improve flow, but Ohno was going to need even more if Toyota was going to be a competitor in the world market. They needed to improve every aspect of their operations faster than anyone else, so Ohno created the Kata process, a systematic approach to continuous improvement that engages the entire organization (Rother, 2010). It is based on the scientific method of defining the problem, proposing a hypothesis for improvement, implementing the change, and monitoring the result of the change to see if it had the desired effect. This approach works very well in manufacturing when the goal is to improve the process used to create the same product over and over again.

This systematic approach of continuous improvement has been broadly studied and engrained in manufacturing as the Lean Six Sigma approach. You can get training and certification in Lean Six Sigma, and it is broadly recognized as the approach for systematically driving improvements in manufacturing and beyond. Manufacturing learned this training requires more than just making sure you can understand the concepts. Higher level certifications with Six Sigma Green Belt, Black Belt, and Master Black Belt require you to demonstrate you can successfully apply the principles on the job to deliver business improvements. Certification requires successful completion of an improvement initiative using the principles with documented results.

With the Kata process, Taiichi Ohno made sure he was able to engage everyone in the continuous improvement process all the way down to the factory worker. The manager's role was to help train everyone in the process and ensure they were using the scientific method. There were very specific steps that everyone was expected to follow that included documenting the plans with what they call the A3 report template because everything can be summarized on an A3 size sheet of paper like in Figure 1 on page 8 (Sobeck and Smalley 2008, 33).

The Toyota production system and the Kata approach got everyone focused on continuous improvement. It was everyone's job to identify problems and engage in getting them fixed. On their production lines, they installed Andon Cords that enabled

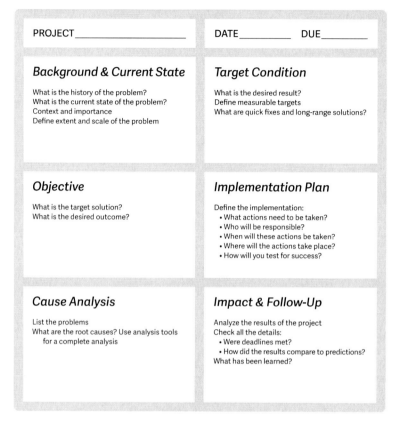

Figure 1: A3 Process Improvement Report

anyone who saw a problem to pull the cord and stop the line so they could fix the process. This was important because if there was a process problem, they wanted it fixed immediately before the process started creating additional defective products that would have to be reworked.

Theory of Constraints

Goldratt was a real champion of Lean Six Sigma and the impact it could have on improving processes. He took it one step further by showing that improvements not focused on the constraint or bottleneck in the process will not improve the flow of the overall system. His Theory of Constraints approach was the answer to this problem (Goldratt and Cox 2004, 360). It ensures that the improvements are focused on addressing the bottleneck by using five focusing steps.

1. Identify the system constraint.
2. Decide how to exploit the system constraint.
3. Subordinate everything else to above decisions.
4. Elevate the constraint.
5. If in the previous steps a constraint has been broken, go back to step one but do not allow the inertia to cause a system constraint.

This is a very systematic approach for continuous improvement that focuses on improving the flow of value through an organization that can be applied broadly beyond manufacturing. A great example of this is presented in the book *The Goal*, which is the model Gene Kim et al., used for writing the IT example in their book *The Phoenix Project*.

Embracing New Capabilities

In *Beyond the Goal: Theory of Constraints*, Goldratt demonstrated how to deal with fundamentally new capabilities. When you introduce new capabilities, you need to evaluate the rules that were based on the previous capabilities and be willing to change those rules to exploit the new capabilities (Goldratt 2005, chap. 1). He used the example of rolling out software for material requirements planning (MRP) to highlight the approach. MRP tries to figure out how much material to order and how much of everything to manufacture based on orders and inventories. Before software, calculating how much to order and how much to build for the next month was a very labor-intensive process. Organizations would run this process once a month. Factories of 300 people would traditionally have around 20 people just to run these calculations. When software came along, this was one of its first applications because these are the types of calculations computers and software can do very well. The computer could easily run all the MRP calculations overnight.

Black & Decker was one of the first companies to rollout MRP systems. They saw dramatic improvements in their ability to commit to new orders while running with historically low levels of inventory. Their responsiveness to their customers increased as a result. The interesting thing was as MRP rolled out to more and more organizations, those organizations weren't seeing the same results. They were spending millions of dollars rolling out these MRP systems, and the lack of results was frustrating. Goldratt examined the rollouts and the discoveries the organizations made. What he found was that there was a fundamental rule from the old system that had not changed. People had simply incorporated the old rule into the new capability. They had not changed how often they ran MRP even though it was now less labor intensive. They were still only running it once a month. This is very different from Black & Decker's practice of efficiently running this process on an ongoing basis. They were planning and running MRP several times a week and optimizing what they built based on current orders and inventory levels. They were much more responsive to their customers and had less inventory than the rest of the industry because once they changed their capabilities, they changed the rules to take advantage of those new capabilities. Where other organizations just saw productivity improvements for their planning process they ran once a month, Black & Decker fundamentally changed the responsiveness of their entire organization by using this capability more frequently.

These examples from manufacturing show the value of using systematic approaches to continuous improvements and provide concepts that we can leverage for our digital world.

Product Development and Design

The way that manufacturing organizations develop products has dramatically improved over time. As the organizations learned more, they came to develop what is known as the stage-gate R&D process for product development. In this approach, product development goes through different phases, with gates that must be passed through before moving on to the next stage. These gates are important because when you move from one stage to another, the expenses that you're committing and the cost of changing goes up significantly. Knowing that the design is going to work and be effective is important to ensure that things are ready before you make the next level of investment. The next step in product development and design that builds from the stage-gate process is the design of the supply chain. Both of these processes are explained below.

Stage-Gate R&D Process

In the stage-gate process, phases are implemented with a gate at the end of each one to ensure the objectives were properly met. The exact stages and gates are fine-tuned for different companies and products, but the concepts are similar. Most start with a phase of investigation where you investigate the idea of a product. This involves some market research and clearly defining the product on paper before deciding to build anything. The next phase could be something like lab prototype, where you build a prototype of a product through whatever manual means you have to see if you can actually design something that works. If you can prove the ability to create a feasible product, then you pass that gate into a phase like production prototype, where the goal is to demonstrate that it can be manufactured with a process that can scale. If this is proved successful and passes the associated gate, then it is okay to start building the product at volume for sale.

This stage-gate process was developed because at each gate there is a significant increase in the commitment of capital, and it becomes harder to change the product design. In the investigation phase, it is just paper and the people working on the plan. In the lab prototype phase, building and testing a prototype gets more expensive, so there are strong incentives to ensure the product is likely to be successful. The production prototype phase brings the investment and risk to a higher level with the creation of capital-intensive manufacturing processes. With the manufacturing release, there is a commitment to build a large amount of inventory that has to be sold, reworked if there is a quality problem, or scrapped if there is not a market. Therefore, the manufacturing industry created this process to minimize risk and increase the likelihood of success by putting gates in between the stages.

The manufacturing product development process has started to change a little bit and become more agile with things like 3D printing to enable prototypes to happen more quickly. Currently, however, 3D printing is still not to the point where it is being used much for high volume production, so at some point there is going to be a big investment in the production level capabilities. So, while there are things being done in manufacturing to make it more nimble and agile, there still are these separate phases that you must go through where you're committing more resources. As a result, you need to be careful, and the stage-gate process was designed to minimize those risks.

Design of the Supply Chain

Once the product is designed with the bill of materials as shown in Figure 2 on page 13, the next step is sourcing all the parts, figuring out how to build the parts, and how and where they can be put together. The bill of materials defines all the parts, how they will be assembled, and the path to the final customer.

The design of the supply chain has a big impact on the flow of product to the customers. For Henry Ford, that meant building one product and providing any color you wanted as long as that color was black—it was pretty straightforward. For today's worldwide economy where individuals would prefer more customization of the product, this is a little more complex. If you're going to manufacture a product in the lowest cost region,

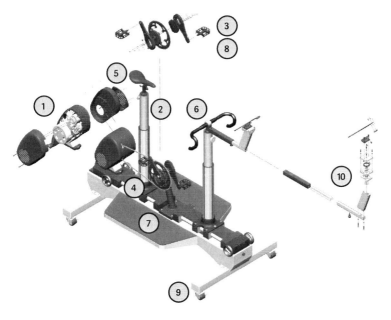

ITEM	PART	DESC	MATERIAL	QTY
1	Gear box	Ten gear		1
2	Telescope post	Adjustable seat post	Alloy	1
3	Pedal		Carbon	2
4	Chain	Link chain	Alloy	1
5	Seat	Racing	Foam	2
6	Handlebars	Swoop	Carbon	1
7	Frame	Adjustable	Aluminum	1
8	Crank		Aluminum	1
9	Wheels	Moving wheels	Alloy	4
10	Display	Interface and display		1

Figure 2: Manufacturing Product Design and Bill of Materials

but you're going to sell it with different customizations in different parts of the world, it is important to design how that is going to work. The supply chain design is that process. The goal is to find the right balance between manufacturing costs, inventory, responsiveness, and availability. The more the demand can be aggregated to a common point in the supply chain, the less variability exists. For example, the worldwide demand for a product is

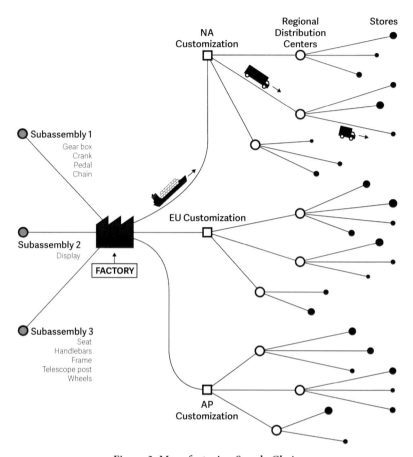

Figure 3: Manufacturing Supply Chain

going to have less variability than individual regions because each region's variability tends to offset other regions' variability. The closer you get to the customer and individual stores, the more variability exists. This is important because the amount of inventory and manufacturing capacity that needs to be held to ensure a given level of availability depends on the demand variability and the time it takes to respond to changes in demand. In a lot of cases, you try to localize or customize the product as close to the customers as you can for quicker response to changes in demand as shown in Figure 3 above. Manufacturing organizations spend a lot of time figuring out where to build base products, where to customize solutions, and where to hold inventory with their supply chain designs. The goal is to maximize the product availability with the least amount of inventory by aggregating demand variability at a common node and doing customizations as close to the customer as possible.

In manufacturing, the way you design the product has broad implications on the lifetime cost and capabilities of the product. This is addressed systematically with DFX, which is designed for different capabilities generically referred to as X. It started with "design for manufacturability," which means pulling in manufacturing engineers earlier in the design process to help design the product so it is as easy as possible to manufacture. There is also "design for quality." The product can be designed in such a way that it's either easier or harder to build in quality. Other concepts are "design for serviceability" and "design for supply chain." The concept of DFX really focuses on the idea that the design of the product has broad implications on the lifetime cost and efficiencies. Therefore, manufacturing has incorporated DFX as a systematic approach to ensuring these broader implications are addressed during the product design phase.

Summary

Manufacturing has a long history of creating systematic approaches to improving how it develops and manufactures products, which have had a significant impact on the effectiveness of the improvements. Using a suboptimal approach like cost accounting was proven to be detrimental to the effectiveness of organizations. The implication for software is that it should be able to achieve similar benefits from systematic approaches as long as we pick the right ones and the industry stays focused on continually improving them. There is a lot that software can learn from the manufacturing processes that have proven over the years to be effective, but those approaches can't simply be copied wholesale. Software is different. The systematic approaches that will work best for software need to be modified to address its unique capabilities and characteristics. In the next chapter, we will review a brief history of software improvements, including the new approaches designed to work specifically for software.

CHAPTER 2

The History of Software Development

When we look at the history of product development and process improvements in the software industry, we can see that, while there isn't the same long and extensive history as in manufacturing, there has been an evolution of approaches. The software industry started by leveraging techniques from manufacturing because that is all that existed. Then, over time, leaders in the software industry started trying different approaches because they realized the traditional techniques were not working very well.

The software industry started by using the stage-gate R&D approach for product development. Instead of an investigation phase and lab prototype phase like in manufacturing, software broke this down into what is commonly referred to as the software product life cycle. The typical phases in the lifecycle are requirements, design, implementation, verification, and maintenance. This focus on the software product lifecycle is known as the waterfall methodology, and it was used for an extensive number of years. Unfortunately, it had a very poor track record. The software projects that used this approach were typically late, over budget, and didn't deliver planned features. To address these issues, the industry thought they needed to get much better at the product life cycle because it seemed like software was just not very good at product development. They tried to implement more processes to do a much better job of documenting in detail the requirements and getting sign-off on those delivery commitments. Adding more and more processes was the way they tried to fix the challenges they were having with software development. Over time, several key people in the software industry realized that this wasn't working very well.

Agile

There were a lot of different groups trying different techniques to address the unique characteristics and capabilities of software. In 2001, leaders from those groups came together at Snowbird in Utah to do a little skiing and see if they could agree on how to approach product development for software (Highsmith 2001). There were leaders from the Scrum Group, the Extreme Programming Group, the DSDM, Adaptive Software Development, Crystal, Feature-Driven Programming, Pragmatic Programming, and they were all looking to see if there was any commonality. They were surprised when they found they had some fairly good alignment on basic principles. They captured this alignment in what they called the *Agile Manifesto*, reproduced on page 19.

These leaders recognized that it really wasn't helping to try to add more and more process to the software development life cycle. Instead, they valued the individuals and interactions over process and tools. They valued working software over comprehensive documentation. They realized that you can add process and get sign-off on your requirements, but when you start writing software, you're going to get more insights into how it should really work. With software, unlike in manufacturing, you don't have to document how the design is going to work and then build the manufacturing line. You can start building the software from the very first line of code. This unique capability enables you to get working software out in front of the user for feedback instead of just going deeper and deeper in the inflexible comprehensive documentation that doesn't change at

MANIFESTO FOR AGILE SOFTWARE DEVELOPMENT

We are uncovering better ways of developing software by doing it and helping others to do it. Through this work we have come to value:

Individuals and interactions over processes and tools
Working software over comprehensive documentation
Customer collaboration over contract negotiation
Responding to change over following a plan

That is, while there is value in the items on the right, we value items on the left more.

Kent Beck	James Grenning	Robert C. Martin
Mike Beedle	Jim Highsmith	Steve Mellor
Arie van Bennekum	Andrew Hunt	Ken Schwaber
Alistair Cockburn	Ron Jeffries	Jeff Sutherland
Ward Cunningham	Jon Kern	Dave Thomas
Martin Fowler	Brian Marick	

©2001, the above authors
this declaration may be freely copied in any form,
but only in its entirety through this notice.

the rate of the software. The other basic principle in the *Agile Manifesto* was placing emphasis on customer collaboration over contract negotiations. This helps to address the fact that 50% of software is either never used or doesn't meet its business intent (Kohavi et al. 2009, sec. 5). Instead of spending a lot of time locking down in a contract exactly what should be delivered, it's more important to get something users can try out to see if it really meets their needs. This idea of responding to change rather than following a plan starts to address a unique characteristic of software: while it is much more difficult to accurately plan, it is also much easier to change. The concepts captured in the

Agile Manifesto were a fundamental breakthrough. It worked to address the unique capabilities and characteristics of software rather than trying to manage it the same way that everything else had been managed.

A lot of people saw great results using Agile principles, and those principles were applied in more and more companies. Over time, the Agile community tried to get much more structured in their approach, and there was training to get certified in Agile. This and almost all training in software to date is focused on being able to prove you understand the concepts and practices. It has not yet evolved like manufacturing where being able to demostrate you can apply the principles to delivery improvements is required. These were all good improvements that helped how software was being developed, but eventually, concern developed that people were becoming so focused on these practices or rituals that they were losing track of the overall principles.

Lean Software Development

In 2003, Mary Poppendieck and Tom Poppendieck published their book *Lean Software Development: An Agile Toolkit*. In the book, Mary takes a lot of her experiences from growing up in a manufacturing environment at 3M and using Lean Six Sigma approaches to improving processes and applies those same concepts to software (Poppendieck and Poppendieck 2003). She uses the principles of Lean manufacturing to help define the Lean principles for software, and she goes beyond the rituals of Agile to the fundamental principles that support the Agile practices. The focus is more on eliminating waste and improving flow for delivering business results than on making sure you are doing Agile correctly.

DevOps

DevOps represented the next big change to software development. The motivation for this concept started with John Allspaw's presentation at the Velocity conference in 2009, when he showed how at Flickr that they were able to release software more often than anyone thought possible (Edwards 2012). Patrick Debois was so excited about the idea that he formed a conference dedicated to moving the concepts forward and coined the term DevOps when he put together his first devopsdays. In 2011, Jez Humble and David Farley published their book, *Continuous Delivery: Reliable Software Releases through Build, Test, and Deployment Automation*, which defined a lot of the technical approaches that enabled these types of improvements.

DevOps started as a collection of different things that organizations were doing to be more effective at delivering on an ongoing basis. What was lacking a bit was a clear definition of DevOps. Gene Kim has added a lot of value to the DevOps community by pulling people together to share ideas during his DevOps Enterprise Summit that he started in 2014. His definition of DevOps is valuable to our ongoing discussion here:

> "DevOps should be defined by the outcomes. It is those sets of cultural norms and technology practices that enable the fast flow of planned work from, among other things, development through tests into operations, while preserving world class reliability, operation, and security. DevOps is not about what you do, but what your outcomes are. So many things that we associate with DevOps, such as communication and culture, fit underneath this very broad umbrella of beliefs and practices." (Gruver 2016, 8)

Gene's definition helps clarify the concepts explored in this book. It's not about the process or tools or any independent element; it's about everything an organization needs to do to succeed in software development from process, tools, culture, change, management, etc., that enables delivery of code on a more frequent basis while maintaining all aspects of quality. A lot of this is nothing more than the Agile principle of releasing code to customers on a more frequent basis—a principal that got left behind as Agile scaled in enterprise because it was hard to scale and beyond the scope of the teams.

From my perspective, one of the big things that enabled DevOps was automation. It was some of the approaches that John Allspaw and others used to create frequent deployments at Flickr. It was the ideas that Jez Humble and David Farley covered in *Continuous Delivery*. These new approaches enabled some real breakthroughs in how we develop and deliver software. But as Goldratt taught us in *Beyond the Goal*, if you roll out a fundamental capability change, and you're not willing to change the rules, you won't achieve the breakthroughs that are possible with the new capability. You need to change how people work and focus on the culture to get the results you want. DevOps started to capture and explore that overall perspective by including everything that enabled organizations to take advantage of the significant breakthroughs.

Project to Product

IT tends to manage software development the same way that organizations manage other capital assets. There's a schedule for delivering the new asset, and when that goal is met, the software goes into maintenance mode. What we have found with this capital-budget-based approach in IT is that teams formed to develop this software would get disbanded and then formed into new teams for the next capital project. The challenge with this approach is that when the teams knew they weren't going to be around to support and use the process on an ongoing basis, they tended to build up a lot of technical debt. They didn't create the processes and approaches that made it easy to maintain the application over a long period of time or to be stable in production. They didn't make a lot of effort to create a supportable process because they were not going to be around for that phase. There was no incentive to automate their deployment pipeline. They were measured by how much business value they could deliver with the budget and time allowed, and so that was their focus. They only had to do it once and get it out the door. Therefore, it wasn't worth investing the time and energy necessary to make sure that they created an efficient flow of value through the organization. They tended to overlook the fact that one of the key advantages of software is that the product can be continually improved over time, so it is important to address the technical problems that are slowing down the flow of value through the deployment pipeline.

Leading edge IT organizations are moving away from managing software as projects and toward funding stable product teams. The goal is to address some of the short-term thinking associated with teams that are formed just for the duration of the project. The product teams are stable over time and responsible for the continuous improvement of the product and the deployment pipeline. Since they will be using the deployment pipeline every day, they are much more likely to invest in things like test automation and work to avoid creating a lot of technical debt. They are also much more interested in learning which capabilities the customers are using and how the product can be continually improved to meet the business intent (Narayan 2018).

Summary

Over time, software organizations have really started to modify their approaches and practices to embrace the unique characteristics and capabilities of software. We've made some great improvements. All these steps were steps in the right direction that are adding value. But when we look at this relative to manufacturing, it's still fairly early in the process, and we don't quite have the same level of engineering rigor and structure necessary for systematically improving how we develop software. We can learn from manufacturing, but we can't just copy them because software is different. The first step in learning how to leverage these improvements is really taking the time to understand in detail the unique characteristics and capabilities of software, which we will cover in the next chapter.

Unique Characteristics and Capabilities of Software

The accomplishments that the thought leaders in manufacturing achieved by creating a systematic approach to improving how they developed both products and processes serves as a good starting point for discussing software product and process development. It is important to understand, however, that software has some very unique characteristics and capabilities that require taking a different approach. The type of work that you do in software development is different from manufacturing in many ways. Software is a digital asset instead of a physical asset, which has some significant implications. Additionally, software development is relatively new compared to manufacturing, so the technologies and processes are less mature. This chapter will provide more details about the differences between software and manufacturing and will help create the framework for later chapters where developing a systematic approach for improving software is the goal. It is important that we understand and appreciate these differences as we develop approaches using certain manufacturing principles optimized to work for software.

Type of Work

The type of work that we do in software is very different from that done in manufacturing. Additionally, there are different types of work within software that require unique and different approaches for improvement.

The creation and development of new products and features in software is one type of work. Most of this is work is very manual and creative. It is written by individuals collaborating with the business to develop solutions to meet the business's needs. It is similar to the early days of manufacturing when everything was manual. Software is more of a craft that is learned over time than an automated manufacturing process that needs to be controlled. Just like with the apprentice approach in manufacturing, improvement in this type of software work requires providing ongoing feedback to help developers improve.

The second type of work that we do in software development is triage and defect fixing. This is very unique to software development. It can be hard to see defects in digital assets, so triage is difficult as a result. A lot of large organizations that I work with, in fact, spend more time and effort in triage and defect fixing than they do writing the code in the first place. Therefore, one of the biggest opportunities for significant improvements in software is making triage and defect fixing work more productive.

The next type of work that happens in large software organizations is repetitive tasks. These include things like building the code, creating an environment, deploying the code, and testing the code. These repetitive tasks are known as the deployment pipeline. The deployment pipeline is the manufacturing process for software where we take everything that's been written and then assemble it and get it ready to ship. This is one area of software where manufacturing techniques can be leveraged. In manufacturing, repetitive tasks tend to be automated to ensure stability. For software development, there is a real opportunity for automating these repetitive tasks. The automation creates consistency so that you do not have to triage defects from manual errors. It also reduces the time and costs associated with these tasks, which enables them to be run on a more frequent basis. The types of things that you do to address repetitive tasks are very different than the types of things that you do to address improving the effectiveness of triage and defect fixing, which are also very different from the types of things that you do to improve the manual creation of code in the first place.

There are also repetitive tasks that occur during ongoing operations. Google's book, *Site Reliability Engineering: How Google Runs Production Systems*, did a really good job of providing examples and opportunities to show how to use automation of repetitive tasks to improve the operations of software (Beyer et al. 2016, chap. 5). Automation frees software workers from mundane work, thus enabling them to do more software engineering work and making them more productive over time.

Digital versus Physical

In software, we're dealing with digital assets instead of the physical assets in manufacturing. That has a lot of broad implications.

With physical assets, creating and manufacturing prototypes is an expensive process that takes a lot of time. This is changing a bit with 3D printing, but physical products are still slower and more expensive to build than software. With software, the manufacturing process of creating an environment, building the code, deploying the code, and testing it is very easy from the beginning. Therefore, for software development, you really don't need to have a line between when you're developing and when you're manufacturing the product with the deployment pipeline. This means you can use the manufacturing process for creating the product from the very first line of code and continue to use it as you modify the product over time.

Additionally, there is no finished goods inventory with software. Because it's digital, you can make as many copies as you want, and you don't have to worry about building up a lot of finished goods inventory. For each change in the software product, you can do a full manufacturing build, release it, and have it ready for customers. This is important because 50% of the time what we thought we were going to achieve with software ends up either never being used or not meeting the original business intent (Kohavi et al. 2009, sec. 5). Being able to manufacture from the beginning and change the product whenever you want is really helpful when you're trying to determine what the customers will use and ensure it will achieve the desired business objectives.

Another thing that's unique to software due to its digital nature is that it is hard to see. With physical assets, you can walk into the factory and see inventory building up on the floor. You can look at two pieces being assembled together and figure out if there is a quality problem because they don't fit together well. In comparison, there is a real lack of visibility with software.

The other way that software is unique and different from manufacturing is apparent when it is viewed from a process standpoint. Manufacturing is trying to build the same thing over and over again with as little variability as possible. With software, every time you run your manufacturing process of creating an environment, building the code, deploying the code, and running the tests, the product is changed. This has broad implications when using the scientific method for continuous process improvement because you're changing both the product and the process at the same time.

Software is also unique in that once you've got the repetitive tasks automated and stable, the primary things that you're trying to find are product defects caused by manual work. Somebody has coded something in such a way that had an implication that you didn't understand and that has created a product defect. This is very different from manufacturing where the process typically creates the product defect. In software, it is the manual creative work of coding that is creating the defects.

The next significant challenge with software is that you're changing the product with every cycle of the process. This is very different from the focus of process engineering in manufacturing where the goal is to create the same product over and over again with limited variability. With software, the additional challenge is ensuring not only that the process is stable, but also that the process can change at the same rate as the product.

Software Maturity

Software is a relatively new process and product, unlike manufacturing. Because software is new, there are a lot of things that are changing very quickly. Having worked in manufacturing and product development, one of the things that I became aware of after moving over into software is the difficulty of planning and predicting software schedules. This is something that I intuitively learned, and it really hit home with me when I spent some time with Martin Fowler. He is one of the authors of the Agile Manifesto and has been working in software his entire career. His wife is a civil engineer. He kept trying to describe the challenges of software engineering to her and finally came up with a good description: It's like the properties of concrete are changing every two years, but you need to create a design and schedule for building the Hoover Dam. It becomes impossible to create the design and schedule because of all the ways concrete is constantly changing. This way of seeing it is closer to the realities of the rate of change in software. Something as fundamental as the languages used for writing software is changing very rapidly.

Figure 4 on page 30 shows the amount of change on just one of the 50 most popular languages that Éric Lévénez's tracks on his website. (Lévénez 2018). This graphic is truncated so the content is visible in the book format. Even in this truncated form it shows just how rapidly something as basic as the languages used for writing software change. This level of change limits the amount of history that developers can use as a baseline for accurately estimating schedules.

The processes used for software development are also changing rapidly. Agile was only introduced as a concept in 2001. Some of the basic principles behind DevOps were not introduced until Jez Humble and David Farley released their book on

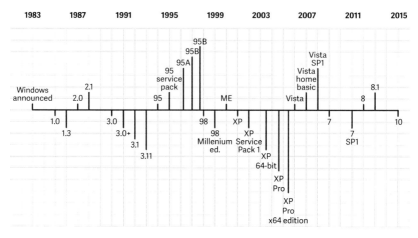

Figure 4: History of changes for Windows programing Language

continuous delivery in 2011. And, as always, adoption has lagged behind the public discussion of these approaches. Additionally, the tools for automating the repetitive tasks in software are fairly new and evolving as shown in Figure 5 below.

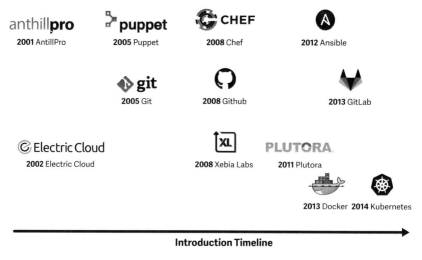

Introduction Timeline

Figure 5: History of DevOps Tools

It is not that people working in software are bad at planning relative to their peers. It is really that everything is changing so rapidly on so many fronts that accurate planning is just that much harder.

Virtualization and Automation

There are a couple of fairly recent, big changes that are having a dramatic effect on software: virtualization of hardware and automation of repetitive tasks.

Virtualization of hardware has separated even more the physical and the digital assets. Before the virtualization of hardware, when you planned the software product, you also needed to bring in the specific hardware for the project, so incorporating lead times for the physical assets was essential. The virtualization of hardware has changed all that. The physical assets required for the software can now be made available on demand either as interchangeable capacity in an internal datacenter or in the cloud. It was a bit like the change to interchangeable parts in manufacturing that enabled significant breakthroughs. The virtualization of hardware has enabled additional decoupling of physical assets and allows more of the flexibility that digital assets provide.

The other big breakthrough to come about recently is the automation of repetitive tasks. This came from few different places. The presentation John Allspaw gave at the Velocity conference in 2009 showed how often they were able to deploy code into production using automation. Then, in 2011, Jez Humble and David Farley came out with their seminal book on continuous delivery, which really set the groundwork for being able to automate a lot of these repetitive tasks. These types of ideas weren't available in the industry before then, and they have a broad implication for how software is developed.

The level of changes in software across languages, processes, and tools is very high compared to other technologies. This means we have less history using the latest approaches as a baseline for estimating schedules for new software projects. This results in planning for software being less accurate than we are used to for more mature technologies.

Summary

Software is different than physical assets. There's a lot we can learn from manufacturing, but the type of work we do is different. The fact that we're dealing with digital assets versus physical ones and the fact that we're dealing with a relatively immature process or technology that's evolving at a very high rate has broad implications across the system. So, when we look at software and try to come up with a systematic approach for how we make improvements, we can learn from manufacturing, but we also need to incorporate the existing differences. The next four chapters will cover how we incorporate those differences in the improvement process in more detail. We'll look at it from four different perspectives, starting with product design and development.

CHAPTER 4

Product Design and Development

The roots of traditional software product development started with the stage-gate R&D process that was developed for physical products. This approach makes perfect sense for those products, but as we will see through reviewing the unique characteristics and capabilities of software, it does not work as well for digital products.

For software, we need to be improving how we design and build the product during development because it impacts the productivity of the development process. This is very different from physical products that have very distinct phases between product development and manufacturing optimization. For software, we need to optimize the product and process during the development process, and we need to focus on product design and manufacturing flow at the same time.

Physical and digital products are similar in that the application and how the product is designed have broad implications for how it is manufactured. Manufacturing understood this a long time ago and developed a systematic approach to addressing those issues with DFX. In this chapter, we will review how manufacturing moves from product design to the manufacturing process to design of the supply chain. We will show how these same concepts can be applied to software when moving from product design or architecture to the manufacturing process or deployment pipeline. We will also show how the design of the product and its application defines the deployment pipeline, which impacts development efficiencies. This is a new way of thinking about software design and its implications on the lifetime costs of the product.

The first step in creating a systematic approach for improving software development is making the product and manufacturing process visible. This provides the basis for how we implement the improvement principles. We will show how the architecture and applications define the deployment pipeline. In manufacturing, different applications require different approaches for applying the principles. The same is true for software, so the first step is clarifying the type of problem we are trying to solve by making the product design and the manufacturing process visible. The deployment pipeline and approaches for improvement will be different for loosely coupled systems, tightly coupled systems, and embedded products. It will also depend a lot on who controls the deployment process. In this chapter, we will lay out how to make this visible so we have the foundation for how to apply the improvement principles to specific applications in subsequent chapters.

Manufacturing Approach to Product Design and Development

As Chapter 1 explores, product development in manufacturing is driven by the stage-gate R&D process because the costs and the risks go up dramatically at different stages of development. This may sound obvious. But the magnitude of the differences and the implications for software are probably not fully appreciated by those who have spent most of their career in software. Therefore, we will start with an example from my career, where the stage-gate R&D process provided some significant advantages.

THE SIDEWINDER CASE STUDY

Single function printers maintained a dominant position in the Enterprise as the means for printing. This all started to change in the early 2000's when copiers became capable of being connected to the network and customers could also print on a copier. At that time, the company I was working for was trying to figure out how to best address that threat and started off by creating a product that tried to provide more of the copier capabilities on our mid range printers. For the first attempt as shown to the right we took a light-weight scanner off of an inkjet printer and attached it to a mid range printer. We also added a control panel and a keyboard to enable us to input information.

That product was launched with limited success. As we researched to understand the problem we came back with a few conclusions. First, was that the scanner was not robust enough to match the print speed which is not the case for copiers. Second, the control panel was too small to be effectively used as a copier replacement. Third, there wasn't the basic paper handling capability of a stapler included in the product. So, for the next generation, we developed a plan to address those weaknesses in our product design. We found a scanner that would match the speed of the printer. It was a little bit bigger to enable it to scan at the rate of the printer. We added a stapler in between the printer and scanner that required a little more room. There was also a much larger control panel. As we went through the concept phase of this product, we felt like we had a pretty good product that was ready to take to the market. It was going to address all the feedback that we had received from the customers and was going to be a significant breakthrough for the market.

Since this was a fundamentally new product we decided to do market research during concept phase. We documented the new product specifications in some PowerPoint slides and created a simple foam core mockup of the product design as shown below.

We used this simple concept of our product to do marketing research around the world. In the market research we would sit behind a two-way mirror and have the moderator describe the products specifications. The feedback we received from the customers was very positive. Then we would show them the foam core of the product. In each case as soon as we unveiled the product to the customers the feedback turned very negative. The product had grown into something that being so close to development of product we hadn't fully appreciated. When the scanner got a little bigger and it got set back a little further to make room for the stapler it started looking like a toilet. Every single focused group that we went to, the customers came back and said, "That's so embarrassing. It is a toilet." It got so bad that as we were going through the specification sheets everyone behind the mirror in the later focus groups would start guessing who was going to call it a toilet first.

Needless to say, this was kind of embarrassing and frustrating for us. Some of the engineers that went to the very first focus group came back and figured that there had to be a different

approach. They determined that we could rotate the printer, put the paper out the side, and the scanner directly on top of the print head. This resulted in a product that was much more pleasing to the eye but had the same specification as the original product. The result was the sidewinder product that was our first successful response to the competitive threat of copiers in the Enterprise.

The side-oriented approach was something that we never considered before but came out of marketing feedback in the concept phase. It saved us millions of dollars of product development for something that would have been a marketing flop. We did this at a relatively low cost. We were able to just print out specification sheets and machine down a piece of foam core. With that minimal investment, we were able to find out a lot about the market acceptance of the product.

This may seem counterintuitive for people who are used to software, which is fairly easy to demo, but this is the background that drives the stage-gate R&D process for manufacturing. It is this stage-gate R&D process that formed the foundation of the software development lifecycle and how broader parts of the organization expect product development to be managed. Again, the thought is that if it worked for manufacturing, it should work for software. However, this doesn't take into account that it is easier for software to develop working prototypes and change the product and that the development costs don't go up as dramatically between phases.

The other fundamental in manufacturing is that there is a very distinct phase of product design where you're trying to figure out the best design and how to build the product. Then there's a phase of manufacturing where you're trying to optimize manufacturing of a consistent product.

Once you finalize the design, you have the bill of material with drawings that detail all of the parts and subsystems like in Figure 6 on the next page. The next step is to design the supply chain and the factory. You want to know how every single part is going to be sourced. You want to know how and where it's going to be assembled and how it's going to be distributed. Part of designing the product is working through the design of the supply chain. In manufacturing, you start with the bill of materials and design a supply chain (Figure 7, page 40). The goal is to find the most cost and inventory efficient supply chain design to fulfill customer demand.

Manufacturing product development also has a real focus on DFX because the product design has broad implications on the lifetime costs and the value the product can provide. The focus is on designing for manufacturing, for quality, for serviceability, and for the supply chain, among other things.

Unique Characteristics and Capabilities of Software Related to Product Design and Development

The biggest difference between manufacturing product development and software product development is that software should not have separate phases between product development and manufacturing. The process we use for manufacturing software can be used throughout product development. The deployment pipeline, which is the process to build the software product, is

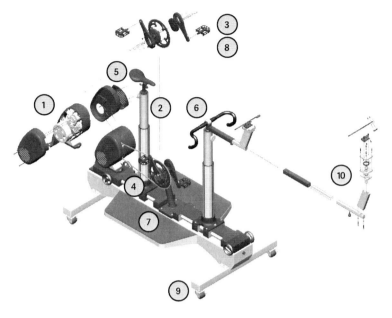

ITEM	PART	DESC	MATERIAL	QTY
1	Gear box	Ten gear		1
2	Telescope post	Adjustable seat post	Alloy	1
3	Pedal		Carbon	2
4	Chain	Link chain	Alloy	1
5	Seat	Racing	Foam	2
6	Handlebars	Swoop	Carbon	1
7	Frame	Adjustable	Aluminum	1
8	Crank		Aluminum	1
9	Wheels	Moving wheels	Alloy	4
10	Display	Interface and display		1

Figure 6: Manufacturing Product Design and Bill of Materials

cheap and easy. There is no worry about building the product often in the early design phases because there is no inventory. Therefore, the process is used from the first line of code. Every time there is a code change, you should be using this same manufacturing process. Additionally we should always be focused on optimizing the deployment pipeline because it has a big impact on the productivity of the organization during development.

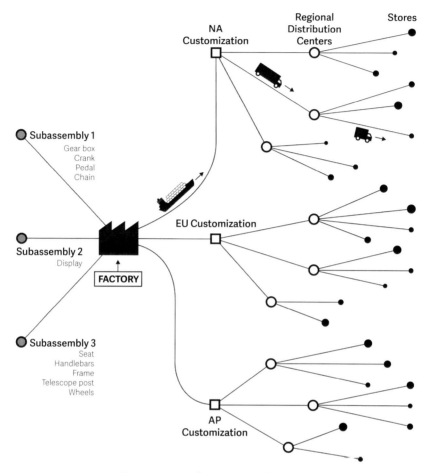

Figure 7: Manufacturing Supply Chain

The ability to continually improve and change the product is important for software because 50% of the software ever developed is either never used or doesn't meet its business intent (Kohavi et al. 2009, sec. 5). To address this, we need to focus not only on developing the product once, but also on the continuous improvement of the product. Getting a product out there and evolving it over time with a process that's efficient is unique to software and helps get us closer to meeting user criteria and business intent.

Software products are digital so there is no finished goods inventory or digital distribution. Once it is built and qualified, you should be able to use it in as many places as required for almost no additional cost. As we design our deployment pipe-lines, we want to ensure we are taking advantage of the unique capability of this digital asset.

Implications for Software Product Development

Manufacturing can provide the basis for our thinking about the approaches we use for product design and development but with modifications to work with software. Even though it's the basis for the software development lifecycle, the stage-gate R&D process doesn't make as much sense for software as we will show below. The concept of DFX is really important, but it isn't considered much by most traditional software organizations. That needs to change. The product application and design has broad implications for the deployment pipeline and lifetime costs for the application. As we will demonstrate, we need to understand these implications for software. The first step is making the product and the software factory visible.

Management of Product Development

Product development for software is very different than it is for manufacturing. Because of these differences, the stage-gate R&D process really doesn't make as much sense. In software, the costs don't rise dramatically at different stages of development. The product is much more flexible and responsive to changes. It's important to understand that software manufacturing can start from the very first line of code and continue to optimize the deployment pipeline and product throughout development. Because we're integrating our code on an ongoing basis, we don't need the planning for integration points to bring everything together.

We need to think of product development and the manufacturing of software with the deployment pipeline as things that are done simultaneously. How you improve the manufacturing of products needs to be brought to bear on how we think about improving the building of code throughout the development process. Instead of measuring software product development the way we measure manufacturing product development, with accuracy to plans and successful completion of gates, we need to start measuring software product development the way we measure the ongoing manufacturing of the product. We need to focus on the flow of value and eliminating waste (covered in more detail in subsequent chapters). We need to apply the Agile principle of working on the most valuable features first, keeping the product close to release quality, and continually improving the product.

DFX

DFX is the other, often overlooked, area where software can benefit from manufacturing principles. Just like in manufacturing, the software product design has broad implications on the lifetime efficiencies and costs of the product. The most important step is to design for the deployment pipeline, including how we deploy to the customer. We also need to design for quality and operations. All of these factors impact the lifetime costs and value of the product. We will start here with design for the deployment pipeline because the application and how the product is designed provides the foundation for how we will apply the principles for systematic improvements. We want to start by making this design and the impact on the deployment pipeline very visible.

Design for Deployment Pipeline

Physical products design for manufacturing and the supply chain because they are aware that the design impacts the efficiency of those processes. Manufacturing starts with the bill of materials that defines all the parts and subassemblies of the product. Based on this design, they then decide where they are going to source all the parts, where they are going to assemble them, and where they are going to hold inventory. There is a lot software can learn from this approach. The bill of materials in manufacturing is the architecture in software. It's the list of all the parts that need to be assembled to create the product. The supply chain in manufacturing is the deployment pipeline in software. This deployment pipeline is used to assemble, qualify, and deploy the product in software.

The product architecture has a significant impact on the deployment pipeline, just like the product design has a significant impact on the supply chain in manufacturing. As we learn from manufacturing, the design of the product and the intent of the manufacturing facility impacts how you address improvements. For Henry Ford, manufacturing a high-volume product with no variability enabled him to use an assembly line with limited space to control inventory as a way to optimize the process. Toyota didn't have the volume for their factories and were manufacturing a wide variety of products, so they needed a fundamentally different approach and used Kanban.

For software, the architecture of the product impacts the deployment pipeline and the approaches to optimization. Different deployment pipelines have different challenges and require different improvement efforts. One of the first steps is to segment the different applications in your organization into different deployment pipelines so you can address their specific challenges. Any group of applications that need to be developed, qualified, and deployed as a system is one deployment pipeline. Any applications that can be released separately and don't have to go through an integrated test environment should be treated as a different deployment pipeline. The reason you segment applications into as many different deployment pipelines as possible is that different deployment pipelines will have unique challenges, and smaller systems are easier to improve. That said, if the applications are tightly coupled in the architecture, you need to treat that as one deployment pipeline, even if it is really big and complex.

The manufacturing supply chain is designed to reduce the impact of demand variability by aggregating inventory and manufacturing capacity at common nodes where there is less variability. In software development, we are trying to aggregate as much common work as possible because we want to take advantage of the ability to build and qualify software once and then use it as many times as possible.

In software product development, this concept is frequently overlooked because most people are thinking about these phases from a product development perspective instead of it in terms of manufacturing code. Additionally, since it's easy and cheap to create the deployment pipeline in software, organizations tend to spin up lots of duplicate work by branching their code. Each time the code is branched, you are essentially creating a new manufacturing line or deployment pipeline. This is something that you'd never do in manufacturing because it's costly and inefficient.

In software, it is also costly and inefficient, just not as much, and it's not as visible to most of the organization. The first step to improving software development is to start making our factories more visible. We need to start with the architecture and document the deployment pipeline. As we will show below, different types of applications and architectures result in very different deployment pipelines that have unique challenges. The first step in applying a systematic approach to improvement requires understanding these differences. This will provide the foundation for how we apply the principles of systematic improvements in later chapters. The table below provides a high level summary of the different product designs and challenges we will cover in more detail next.

Product design implications on deployment pipeline summary

Architecture/Application type	Challenges
Loosely coupled	Most efficient
Tightly coupled	Coordination, quality, and flow
Customized Off-the-Shelf	Deployment, branching, coordination, quality, flow
Embedded software	Hardware & product variability, automated testing, coordination, flow

Loosely Coupled Architecture

The most efficient architecture and deployment pipeline is a loosely coupled system where small teams can independently develop, qualify, and deploy code into production. This is a lot of what you hear talked about in DevOps. These are the organizations that are continually improving the product faster than anybody else because they have the ability to rapidly learn, adjust, and evolve. This very simple deployment pipeline is shown in Figure 8 below. It moves from developers writing code to testing in an environment to rolling straight into production. They control their deployment processes so they can use approaches such as canary releases and A/B testing to get very clear feedback from their customers. They don't have to deal with the overhead of coordinating their release with a lot of other people because the loose coupling of the architecture means they have well-defined interfaces with other teams that are validated with automated testing. They can also risk moving faster with less preproduction testing because if they see an issue during the canary release to a few customers, they can roll back the change and fix the issue without impacting very many people. This is the ideal scenario because it's the simplest most efficient and smooth flow of value from a business idea into the hands of the customer.

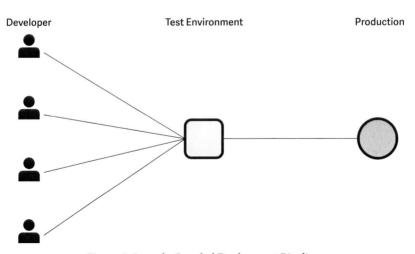

Figure 8: Loosely Coupled Deployment Pipeline

TIGHTLY COUPLED ARCHITECTURE

The second-best architecture and deployment pipeline is a large, tightly coupled system where you still control the deployment process. In this case, being able to deploy independently doesn't work because you've got to coordinate the work across a lot of different teams. The tight coupling means a change in one component can have unknown implications somewhere else in the system. Therefore, you need to test all the components in the tightly coupled architecture together and release them as a system.

Ideally, you would just build and test this enterprise system frequently enough that there are a small number of changes that are easy to triage. The problem is that this is not very practical with large numbers of people working on tightly coupled systems that take time to build, deploy, and test. For these tightly coupled systems, we need a different approach for the deployment pipeline to localize defects and improve the efficiency of triage. This requires breaking the large, tightly coupled system into subsystems. Similar to breaking the bill of materials into subsystems, with tightly coupled architectures you need to break the architecture into smaller components.

When breaking a large system like the one in Figure 9 at left, we need to determine what makes a good subsystem. For this, we look for clean interfaces in the architecture. We also look for organizational boundaries between owners of different applications

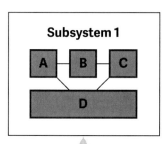

Service Virtualization

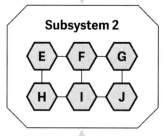

Service Virtualization

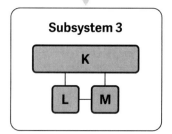

Figure 9: Tightly Coupled Architecture

so we can have clear owners for keeping the subsystem stable. Once we have the subsystems, we make sure we test them and use quality gates to ensure the subsystems are stable before integration into the full system.

Each of these subsystems needs to be assembled and tested and then integrated and tested with the other subsystems like shown by the grapic in Figure 10 of a deployment pipeline for a tightly coupled system. This isn't as good as a loosely coupled system because it requires more time, effort, and coordination (Gruver 2016, chap. 7).

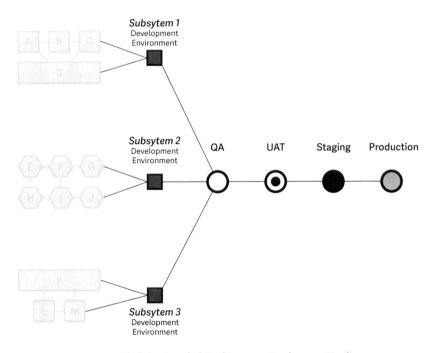

Figure 10: Tightly Coupled Architecture Deplyment Pipeline

More time and effort are required to coordinate all these components and ensure they are ready to release. In fact, for a lot of organizations, the time it takes to test, triage, and fix all the defects is longer than the business is willing to wait for releases. In these situations, organizations address the need for more frequent releases by creating release branches. The number of release branches required and the associated duplicate work depends on how frequently the business needs releases and how long it takes to go from functionality complete to the code having high enough quality for production. For some organizations, this delta is so large that they need to manage multiple release branches at a time with all the associated duplicate work as shown in Figure 11 below. This goes against the unique capability of digital assets to be created once and then used easily in as many places as required. This duplicate work is a big source of waste, so one of the first steps to systematically improving software is making the deployment pipelines and associated branching very visible.

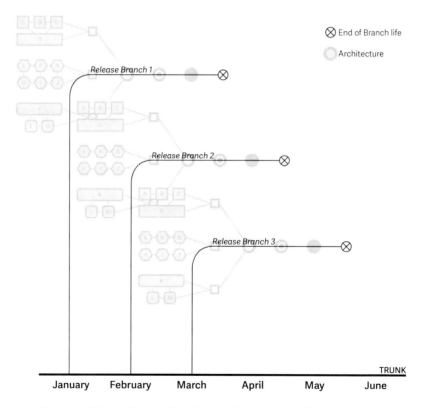

Figure 11: Tightly Coupled Deployment Pipeline Branching Complexity

Customized Off-the-Shelf Software

The next type of applications with a different deployment pipeline are large software applications sold, customized, and then installed in the end user's datacenter. These are large software products, such as manufacturing resource planning, enterprise resource planning, human resources, and application lifecycle management solutions, that have broad applications across many different companies. For these products with broad applications, it doesn't make sense for each company to create their own solution. Development costs can be spread across a lot of different companies, giving each company access to better, less expensive products than they could create on their own. The only downside is that individual companies typically have to make some customizations to the product to enable it to fit their specific business requirements.

This approach does provide economies of scale, but it has effects on the efficiencies of the deployment pipeline for both the companies developing the products and the companies purchasing them. If you are a company developing this software, you have the same challenges that you do with a large, tightly coupled system. In addition, you don't own deployment. In this case, you're very dependent on your customers for when they will deploy the software. Because of that, you can't do canary or A/B testing. This means you need to do a much better job of testing the product before releases. Also, the frequency that you can do continuous improvement iterations on the product is based on the customer's willingness to update to the latest version of the code.

Because upgrading, customizing, and testing are all very hard, the end users don't want to upgrade very often. If they run into an issue or a bug with the version they have installed, they tend to ask the provider for a patch to the current version of software instead of taking the next version that probably already has the fix. This is inefficient for the developer of the customizable software because it requires them to support additional branches and all the inefficiencies associated with that duplicate work. It also slows down the rate at which you can provide additional value to the customer because it is based on how frequently they will update to the newest versions.

It is inefficient for organizations deploying these applications because every time they want an updated version of the product, they have to update the code, implement their customization, and validate that everything is working correctly. If this is as hard and complex as it is with most products, companies are not going to be able to update very frequently, and the continuous improvement process of the software slows way down.

From a deployment pipeline perspective, this is one of the most inefficient models for both the suppliers and the users. The deployment pipeline looks a lot like your large, tightly coupled systems, but as shown in Figure 12 below, it has a much larger number of branches that have to be supported on an ongoing basis. The problem is so pronounced with most providers of these customized applications, that eventually they have to end

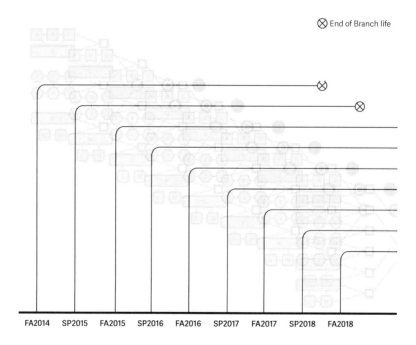

Figure 12: Customized Off-the-Shelf SW Branching complexity

of life a specific version of the code to force customer to a new version. Even when they do that, they still end up supporting lots of different branches to keep their customers happy.

EMBEDDED SOFTWARE

The last type of deployment pipeline dependent on architecture and application is embedded software. This is software running in a product that frequently has custom hardware. There are a lot of different applications like this in the automobile industry. The LaserJet printer and other products also are embedded software applications. In this case, your deployment pipeline typically has software code that can be tested and qualified on a simulator. It also has some low-level firmware that is running on custom hardware which can only be tested with an emulator that has the custom hardware. The deployment pipeline may also need to have more than one type of emulator depending on the different custom hardware that is in different products. Additionally, the final step in the deployment pipeline requires testing on all of the different products.

A typical embedded software deployment pipeline ends up looking something like Figure 13 on page 52. The software that can be tested on a simulator can typically be managed on one common branch with quick feedback and efficient flow. The duplicate work for the low-level firmware depends on the number of custom hardware solutions and the number of different emulators. Finally, if you end up having to test much on the final product, the testing is duplicated across all of the different products that are supported.

Embedded software is another application where you don't usually control the deployment, so you have some of the same challenges as customized, off-the-shelf software. The testing needs to be much more extensive before release. Additionally, your customer base frequently requires you to provide patches on old versions of the software, which requires supporting multiple branches.

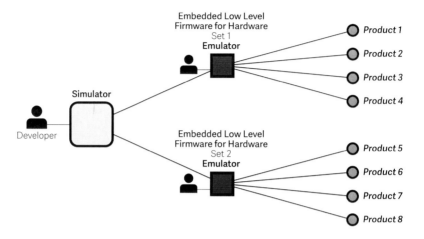

Figure 13: Embedded SW Deployment Pipeline

Design for Quality and Triage

There are other things we can do with design to make software development more efficient. For example, designing for quality is just as important in software as it is in manufacturing. One of the common mistakes organizations make is to design business logic into their user interface (UI), which means that they need to heavily rely on automated UI testing. This automated UI testing tends to be more brittle and difficult to maintain. If they could keep the business logic out of the UI, they could rely on API testing that is much easier to maintain and triage.

The coupling of different components tends to make the triage more challenging. Well-designed interfaces can make developing and maintaining software much easier. Improving software development, as we will see in the next chapter, requires moving to building in quality with automated testing. If we keep this in mind while designing the product, it can make life much easier down the road.

Design for Operations

The product design also has implications for how hard it is to support in production. Because of the complications associated with tightly coupled architectures, the current trend in the industry is to move to micro services that can be independently developed, qualified, and deployed. This provides a lot of advantages for development teams. It works and is easy to manage for very mature operational organizations. But if you're moving into an organization that's not as mature, then you need to figure out the tradeoffs between making the development processes more efficient and adding complexity to your operations group. Loosely coupled systems like micro services are the right way to go in the long run, but you need to make sure you are developing the capabilities to support them in production.

Making the Product and the Software Factory Visible

The first step to setting the foundation for improvements is making the product and the software factory visible. The approach to making these visible is different for existing products than it is for creating new products from the ground up. For existing products, we need to document how it is currently working as discussed below. For new applications, we need to start creating and making the factory visible as soon as we start writing code, as demonstrated in the HP LaserJet example.

Existing Products

The first step is documenting your current architecture and deployment pipeline, including all the branches. We need to make the digital assets as visible as the physical assets so we can start improving them. If the architecture is loosely coupled, that step is pretty simple. If you have a tightly coupled system, it's important to take your architecture and break it down into your deployment pipeline, which is how you assemble and qualify all these subcomponents and the full system. I found the best way to get people to start documenting their deployment pipeline is to have them start with the architecture and then describe the different environments they use for development. That is covered in a lot more detail in my third book,

Starting and Scaling DevOps in the Enterprise, but this idea of being able to document your deployment pipeline is an important first step.

HP LASERJET CASE STUDY

If you are creating a new product, documenting the existing deployment pipeline obviously doesn't work, so you need to start with a different approach (Gruver, Young, and Fulghum 2013, chap. 4). I think the classic example of creating something new is what we did with the re-architecture of the LaserJet firmware. In this case, we were using and improving our deployment pipeline from the very first line of code. We were doing automated builds. We were doing continuous integration of the entire system. We were adding automated tests along the way. In the first phases, we didn't start with a well-defined architecture. We started talking about the easiest things that we could do with the system. In our case, that was creating a scan that we could put on the network. We started by creating a thin slice through the architecture that would work. Our lead architect, Pat Fulghum, would spend time working on different parts of the architecture that needed to be created. He'd send teams to prototype different approaches for that code. He would spend all day in 30-minute increments, having teams at his desk reviewing the implementation that they created and looking at the pros and cons of the various design patterns. He worked with them to come up with the most efficient patterns to be used for the architecture. Writing code and creating a new architecture is a very creative manual process. In manufacturing, they transferred knowledge through the apprentice system. Pat had done already several re-architectures, and he was using this process to transfer his knowledge to the next generation.

We were using the deployment pipeline from the very first line of code. We were using an evolutionary approach to bring up the architecture. When we came to a new place where we had to design, we would try several different approaches to that design until we found the best design pattern for that thin slice of the architecture. Once we had good design patterns, we would replicate the pattern to fill in the corner cases.

We were doing product and process development at the same time. This example shows that with software you can move from an idea where you do product development and then manufacture to using your manufacturing process from the very beginning, while simultaneously optimizing your product and your manufacturing process to gain some dramatic efficiencies.

In my mind, this is the role of the modern architect. It's not just drawing diagrams. It's really about creating design patterns of working code that can show how the architecture is going to work. I like the combination of what Pat was able to do here, because not only was he coming up with the architecture, he was also encouraging people to contribute. People were getting their fingerprints on the design, so they were committed to the implementation.

Summary

As we've shown here, product development for software can and should be very different than it is for manufacturing. The stage-gate R&D process doesn't make as much sense for software because you can start assembling and building the entire product from the very first line of code. Instead, we need to think more about applying approaches for manufacturing physical assets to how the value flows through our deployment pipelines.

With software, the product design and application has broad implications for the lifetime cost and value that you can create out of a product. So, we need to think not only about how the product will be used as we design the product, but also about all the steps between the business idea and how it gets deployed to the customer. Like with manufacturing, we need to ensure the approaches we use for improvement are modified to address the unique challenges of the different applications. The first step is improving the visibility of the product and the deployment pipeline. It lays the foundation for how to apply the improvement principles to specific applications. The next step is addressing the rework associated with defects and poor quality, which we will explore in the next chapter.

CHAPTER 5

Building Quality into the Software Development Process

———————

Manufacturing learned early on that the best way to improve productivity is to build the product right the first time. This realization led to very systematic approaches for addressing quality issues. Since the process was creating the product, manufacturing focused on process control to ensure they were building in quality. For software, it is just as important to build in quality, but the approaches will have to change because the developers are creating a product instead of a process.

In this chapter, we will review how and why manufacturing moved to building in quality. It would be nice if we could leverage all the great work manufacturing has done with quality, but as we will show, software is a very different animal. There isn't the same level of focus on building in quality, and it is much more difficult since we are not building the same product over and over again. In fact, the product changes every time we do a build, so software needs to develop different approaches for building in quality.

Doing this requires developing a stable quality signal, which is a significant journey for most large tightly coupled systems (see the Optum Technology case study). Developers must work differently to build in quality while they are writing the code since it is their work that creates the product. It requires different approaches to controlling quality. Instead of process control charts, we need to create product control charts. The application and the deployment pipeline are going to drive quality expectations. A loosely coupled website that can use canary releases has one set of pre-release quality expectations. Embedded software for medical devices has a completely different set of requirements driving different quality expectations. Additionally, once the stable quality signal is in place, ensuring that the process can change at the rate of the product is much more important than ensuring the process is in control.

Manufacturing Approach to Quality

Manufacturing has a long history of focusing on quality because it doesn't just impact the end result (product), it also has a dramatic effect on the efficiencies of the manufacturing process. They realized early on that they needed to move away from inspecting for quality to building it in if they were going to efficiently manufacture high quality products. They tended to automate repetitive tasks where it made sense because they realized that was much more consistent. With automation, they didn't end up getting the variability that humans typically introduce.

Oncc thcy had things automated, they realized that the process was primarily creating the product. Deming, along with others in the quality movement, focused on improving quality by ensuring that the processes that created the product were in control (Deming 1982, chap. 11). Manufacturing processes have natural variation. Deming would measure that natural variation. If the variation was in tight enough control to create a quality product, then he would create control charts for the process and continue to run the manufacturing process as long as it stayed within those control limits. If it went outside of the control limits of natural variation, he knew something had fundamentally changed and that he needed to figure out the problem and address it to get the process back in control. If the process had too much natural variation to create a quality product, he would use the scientific method to reduce it. He would measure the variability in the current process, create a hypothesis about what might reduce that variability, run an experiment to validate the hypothesis, and measure the output. He would use this scientific approach to improve the process so it could create a quality product. This ability to control and improve the process is how manufacturing starting building quality into products instead of relying on inspection.

This wasn't necessarily good enough to find all the problems in the system. Occasionally, in final assembly, something would be discovered that created a significant quality problem that hadn't been caught by the process control limits. In this case, it would be necessary to go back and rework the inventory built up in the system and find the process that started creating those quality problems. To address the risk of these quality issues, they tried to limit the amount of inventory in the system. This minimized the risk to rework and reduced the time between when the issue was created and when it was detected.

Unique Characteristics and Capabilities of Software Related to Quality

Probably the biggest difference in quality between manufacturing and software is that in manufacturing, they made the cultural shift to building in quality decades ago. With software, the accepted practice in many circles is still to inspect in quality. We've even designed our product life cycle around periods when we inspect for quality and do rework. We build up large amounts of inventory and batch it into lengthy inspection and rework cycles called hardening or verification.

In software, there are still many manual, repetitive tasks. A lot of large organizations that have begun the DevOps journey have started automating and fixing their repetitive tasks, but the majority of software organizations still haven't automated a significant amount.

In manufacturing, where they are creating the same product over and over again, it is easy to use the scientific method to improve quality. It's as simple as changing the process and analyzing the impact it has on the output to see if your improvement hypothesis was correct. With software, when you're changing both the product and the process at the same time, it's much harder to use the scientific method for process improvement.

Additionally, the signal that we use for quality in software isn't typically a dimension or a tolerance, where you can see variations over time but for the most part software quality depends on pass fail tests. This test passed or it didn't. That's a little bit different with build times and performance where you can see variations over time but for the most part software quality depends on pass fail tests.

The other challenge with software is that it's really hard to see. In manufacturing, we can watch a product coming together and see if there's going to be interference between different parts. In software, it's hard to see quality issues. The primary way that we start to see the product quality in software is with testing. Even then, it is difficult to find the source of the problem.

To get a stable quality signal, we need a repeatable deployment pipeline where we can get consistent results from our test automation. Once you have that in place, the thing causing quality problems with software is not associated with the process that assembled the product but with the manual coding that created the product. As a result, to do quality improvements for software, once we get a stable deployment pipeline, our primary focus needs to shift to how we provide feedback and quality control for the manual coding work. This is very different from the process control approach to building in quality in manufacturing.

Once we have this automated deployment pipeline that's stable, one of our biggest challenges with software is being able to change the process at the same rate as the product because the product is changing in every cycle of the build process.

Implications of Building in Quality for Software

In software, we need to shift from the mindset and philosophy that it's okay to build up large amounts of inventory and inspect in quality later to a real focus on building in quality from the start. This reduces the amount of waste associated with hardening phases and improves flow. It requires a very stable, quality signal that people can react to on an ongoing basis. As I work with lots of different organizations implementing DevOps throughout the world, I have found that putting in place this clear quality signal is one of the biggest challenges. It was a big motivation for writing this book. I have come to the conclusion that we need to step back and take a much more systematic approach to making sure that we're getting a good clear quality signal. Then, as Goldratt taught us, once we have this fundamentally new capability in place, we can start changing the rules to achieve dramatic improvements.

Developing a Stable Quality Signal

We can learn a lot from manufacturing and the use of the scientific method as we try to create a stable process. However, the scientific method doesn't work very well if we're changing too many variables at a time. Therefore, we need to use a systematic approach. The first step in making sure that we have a good quality signal is to pick an environment somewhere along the deployment pipeline to start our work. Ideally, you want to begin as far down or to the right on the deployment pipeline as you have influence in the organization. If you go too far right beyond your level of influence, you will be limited in your ability to implement the changes required to improve stability. If you start too far left, the improvements in stability will only help the limited number of people working on that part of the deployment pipeline. Once we have picked the right environment, we're going to start running experiments to see if we can get a stable quality signal.

The next step in creating a stable quality signal is to take a set of automated tests and run them to check for repeatability. If you don't have any automated tests, it's a good opportunity to write a few. Because our goal is to validate the stability of our tests, we don't want to change too many variables at a time. Therefore, we're going to use the same environment with the same code and the same deployment, and we're going to run all of our automated tests 20 times in a row. We need to capture those results and throw them in a database for analysis. The typical output of the analysis will look like Figure 14 below. You will have some tests that are stable and always passing. You'll have some tests that are finding a known defect and always failing. What I find with most organizations is you also have a lot of tests that are toggling between pass and fail. We can't use the failing tests as a quality signal until we get the associated defect fixed, and we can't use the toggling or flaky tests until we get them fixed. The failing tests and the flaky tests need to be removed until we address the issues because they are just sending a bad signal.

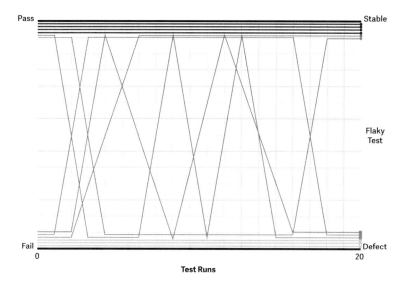

Figure 14: Test Stability Analysis

Next, we need to ensure these stable tests are really stable by running the same tests in random order. Take the results of this test run, put them back in the database, and look at the data to see if there are any additional flaky tests. If there are, we need to add them to the flaky test pile to be reworked. I have yet to work with any organization that has used this process to figure out whether they have a good quality signal that hasn't had to go back and do a significant amount of rework on their automated tests. I have had several organizations argue they need to keep running these flaky tests because they provide code coverage. I strongly disagree. By doing this, you are asking developers to either waste time debugging failures that are not code related or training them to ignore test failures. Our goal here is to get down to a set of reliable tests that we can use to test the rest of the deployment pipeline and to then use as a quality signal that requires developers to respond.

The next step is ensuring that the test environment can handle the load of automated testing. We run as many of these automated tests in parallel against the test environment with the same code and deployment as before. Ideally, all of these tests should pass. This frequently is not the case, however.

There are many different things that can happen in these environments. I have had clients with tens of thousands of automated tests they only run once a week because they need the rest of the week to triage the failures. When we started working to get better stability, they found out that most of the tests were timing out because the environments were sized too small. The engineers spent the first day running the tests and the whole rest of the week debugging and trying to figure out which ones were really failures, all because the environments were too small. To improve the stability in this case, they just need to get a larger system that will run without timing out. I've seen organizations that have flaky load balancers in their test environments that cause test time outs. These types of issues need to be understood and addressed before you can achieve a stable quality signal that you can use to start building in quality. If you don't drive these issues to root cause and get them fixed, any attempt to build in quality will be undermined by this instability.

All of these issues could be going on in your organization now. They're just happening at a frequency that's low enough that people can deal with it. They're using brute force to muscle their way through the issues. As we increase the frequency of these test cycles, though, we need to resolve them once and for all. The process of fixing these issues enables us to build a stable quality signal, but it also immediately starts reducing the amount of friction people have to deal with on a day-to-day basis. Fixing them is going to take some work. You need to find the capacity to do root cause analysis and fix the issues. This step can leverage all the systematic approaches, such as Lean Six Sigma, that manufacturing developed for analyzing and solving stability issues.

Once you know that the environments and the tests are stable, we're going to add one variable at a time to ensure the stability of the entire system, starting with deploy. In this case, we're going to take the same version of code and environment, deploy the code, and run the automated tests, then deploy the code again and run the tests. We're going to do that 20 times and put the results into a database to see if we've still got a stable signal. If not, we need to automate and fix the issues in the deployment process that are causing inconsistency.

Next, we need to ensure there are not any environment issues causing stability problems. In this case, we need 20 cycles of creating the environment, deploying the code, and running the tests. The goal is to see if we can consistently create environments without impacting the stability of the quality signal. If creating new environments starts introducing more instability, we need to address those issues before we start building in quality. To summarize, the steps to a stable quality signal are as follows:

Creating a stable quality signal	
Step 1	Select an environment
Step 2	Validate tests for repeatability
Step 3	Validate tests can run in random order
Step 4	Ensure environment is stable under load
Step 5	Ensure deployment process is stable
Step 6	Ensure environment creation is repeatable

One of the challenges organizations have when they start automating their deployment pipeline and "doing DevOps" is that it is hard to figure out where to start. They want to start with the change that is going to provide the biggest benefit so they can gain positive momentum for the transformation. As we learned from manufacturing, the systematic approach to improvement depends on the application. With software, it also depends on the sources of instability that exist for that specific deployment pipeline. The steps above are provided as a systematic approach to prioritizing the work that is driving instability for your particular application. There is one more thing that we can do to help with the prioritization process and that is effective defect tagging. When we log a defect, we want to know which version of the code and which environment, and we want it tagged for root cause. We want to know if the problem is the code, test, environment, deployment, or database. This enables us to create Pareto charts like Figure 15 on page 66 that we can also use to help prioritize improvements to the deployment pipeline.

This systematic approach to stabilizing and automating the deployment pipeline is going to take a while for most large organizations, but as you can see in the Optum case study below, fixing the issues that have been in your organization for years can start providing benefits right away.

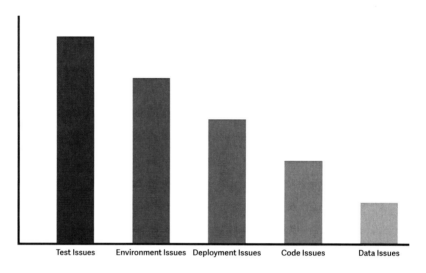

Figure 15: Pareto chart of Defects

OPTUM CASE STUDY

A good example of systematically creating a stable quality signal is Ted Youel's journey at Optum Technology (Youel, Gruver, and Keyes 2018). Ted's team spent a few years going through and addressing all the stability issues in their deployment pipeline. When I first met Ted's team, they had been doing Agile development and test automation for a while. Each of the Agile teams were responsible for delivering new features and test automation every iteration. Their product development process would have five, two-week development sprints. Then they would have a four-week hardening phase where 100% of the team would move from doing feature development to inspecting quality and fixing all the defects. They had created this new test automation capability, but we found that they were only running it at the end of each iteration when they were signing off stories. Then during the hardening phases, they would run the Agile teams feature test automation again, along with automated and manual regression.

They were not running any of the tests on a daily basis. Like so many software organizations, they had the cultural norm of building up large amounts of inventory and then inspecting in quality during the hardening phase. One of the first steps we took was to focus on figuring out how to build more frequently and use the test automation to build in quality. Ted's team worked in a much broader system, so they did all the final testing in an integrated test environment. They realized that when they were trying to run their automated testing frequently, the endpoints from different teams were down or not working as expected. For them to get a stable quality signal, they needed to be able to mock out that instability in the broader system using service virtualization so they could find code issues on their side. They needed to be able to deploy and test on a more frequent basis, which required investments in automation.

It took a while to implement the changes because, like most organizations, everyone was already fully booked delivering new features. But over time, Ted's team found the capacity to make changes and started seeing improvements. Where it used to take 100% of their team to inspect in quality and fix the defects for the four-week hardening phase, in 2017 they found they only needed half the team. They were able to move the other half of the team to the next release and get started earlier.

They continued this journey of systematically improving issues that were impacting the stability of their quality signal over time, as shown in Figure 16 on page 68.

By 2018, they had a stable quality signal they could use for gating code. It required automating most of their deployment pipeline and using service virtualization to isolate their team from the instability in the rest of the system. It also required reworking most of their automated tests because they realized they had a fair amount of stability problems with their current designs. They were using XPath instead of element IDs. They hadn't written their tests from an object-oriented standpoint, so they were having a hard time changing the tests fast enough

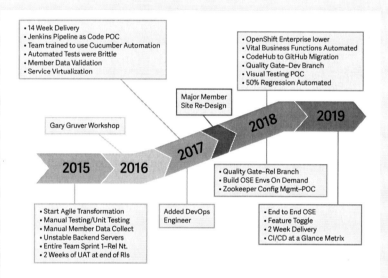

Figure 16: MnR Portals DevOps Journey

to keep up with changes in the product. What they found is that the tests weren't stable enough to be used as a quality signal.

This is typical of most organizations. They have automated tests somewhere in their system, but when they start trying to use them to build in quality, they find they are not stable or maintainable. Most organizations have to rework their test framework and create automated test design patterns that are stable and maintainable before they have a stable quality signal. Therefore, when I work with organizations, I always recommend they start by evaluating their test automation for stability and using it as a quality gate before they write any more tests that will probably end up needing to be reworked.

As Ted went through this journey of improving stability and building in quality, he found it dramatically reduced the amount of waste associated with the hardening phase. Over time, they were able to significantly reduce the amount of time and resources required for triage and fixing defects, as shown in Figure 17 page 69.

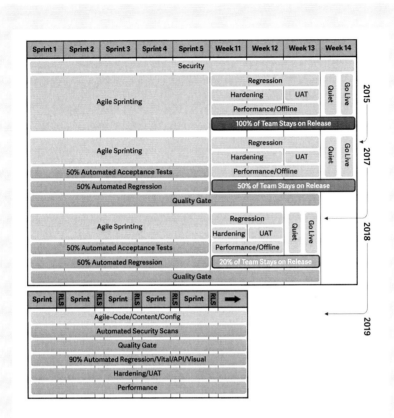

Figure 17: Optum removing harding waste over time

This is a really good example of what it takes to drive stability and the business benefits it can provide. Your journey will be different as your organization is unique, and it is going to vary for different deployment pipelines within your organization. The steps in the journey should be based on the requirements of individual applications and sources of instability. There isn't one path that every organization should follow to reach a level of maturity to ensure success. Like in manufacturing, it is more important to apply the principles and then adjust the practices to address the specific application. The principle of quality is taking a systematic approach to creating a stable signal and then using that signal to build in quality. There's a lot that we can learn from Lean Six Sigma if we're not changing both the product and the process at the same time. Start by finding a set of automated tests that can be used to drive stability across the deployment pipeline. Then take a systematic approach to improving stability across environments, deployments, and tests. Once you create that stability, you can start using that fundamentally new capability to change your approach for how you do development. You can start to build in quality versus inspecting it in the large batch of inventory in the end game.

As Goldratt showed with the MRP system, instead of just automating tests to reduce the cost of testing that are run during the hardening phase, we can use this new capability running automation every day to build in quality. This is how Black & Decker used their MRP implementation to achieve lower inventory and better availability than anyone else. They didn't just improve MRP by automating the manual process. They used the new capability to change how the entire organization worked by adjusting plans multiple times a week when they ran the MRP process on a more frequent basis.

Development Changes Required for Building in Quality

A stable signal enables developers to build in quality. Like with manufacturing, though, it does mean that organizations need to start behaving differently. If they're going to achieve the breakthroughs that are possible, they need to start changing the rules to take advantage of this new capability. Development teams will need to start working differently. They need to think through how they bring code in without breaking existing functionality. They need to move away from modifying the services that will break existing functionality to versioning services so they can make changes to the service without breaking existing functionality. They need to look at using evolutionary database design approaches so they can change their databases in a way that does not break existing functionality (Ambler and Sadalage 2006).

These changes take a while for most organizations, but they are part of fundamentally changing the rules so you can start building in quality.

This approach of building quality with test automation is probably one of the biggest fundamental changes that has happened in software organizations in years. A lot of different organizations have done exactly what happened with the rollout of MRP. They've implemented the new capabilities. They've added some automation, and they've added some environment automation. They've put it under source control. They've done some deployment automation. But they haven't taken that fundamental step toward changing how they do software development by building in quality. That needs to change if they are going to see the dramatic improvements that are possible with this new capability.

Build Acceptance Tests

Once we have this stable deployment pipeline and a clear quality signal, we can start building in quality. As we do this, it's important to understand that, unlike manufacturing, we're not looking for defects created by the process. We are looking for product defects created by manual coding. These are defects in the code written by individuals that had an unintended consequence or impact on the quality of the product. The goal here is two-fold. First, is to find defects as quickly as possible and give feedback to the individual developers while they're working on the code so they can learn from the mistake. Second, is to limit the impact a defect has on the deployment pipeline as much as possible.

One of the biggest challenges with software development is the manual work associated with defect fixing and triage. Ted's team was able to dramatically reduce the waste associated with that process. He did that by getting a clean quality signal and running that signal on a much more frequent basis. By increasing the frequency, there were far fewer changes associated with any test run, which made the debug and test triage much more efficient.

The first step to building in quality is requiring developers to respond to the feedback from the stable quality signal. This will be a learning experience for most development organizations so we will want to start with a reasonable number of tests they can successfully keep passing. These tests are the build acceptance tests. They define the minimal level of quality you will allow in the system. Code commits that break these test will not be allowed on trunk. Keeping these test passing will be a learning experience for most organizations so we want to start with a reasonable quality bar and then raise it over time as developers learn to bring in new functionality without breaking the existing functionality.

These build acceptance tests will come from the automated tests that were part of the stable quality signal. It might not be all of these tests because we need the build acceptance tests to run fast enough to enable the small batch sizes we require for efficient triage. If you have a modern application with good automated unit testing coverage it can be all the tests because well designed unit tests run very fast. If you have a legacy application that is more dependent on slower running API or system tests you are going to have to split the tests into build acceptance tests and regression tests.

The build acccptancc tests are how you build in quality. Code that breaks these tests is not allowed on trunk. These tests are finding defects but instead of dealing with the overhead of logging, tracking, and closing defects we just require the developers to fix the defect and get the build acceptance tests back to passing before their code can stay on trunk. This is how we start building in quality.

Product Quality Control Charts

The product control charts are how we understand the overall quality of the system. For large systems with lots of automated testing we can't run everything in build acceptance testing. The rest of the automated testing is the regression set that needs to be run on a daily basis.

To improve quality, we need to do more than just run in smaller batch sizes and keep the build acceptances tests passing. We need to be able to statistically analyze the stability of our regression testing as well. In this case, we need to create product, as opposed to process, control charts that they have in manufacturing. These product control charts, like Figure 18 below, use test-passing rates to help triage the system and understand overall stability. When we are running a large number of automated tests on a frequent basis, we can't afford to triage every failure. Instead, we want to use the statistical view of passing rates to help triage the system. For this to work well, we need to tag our tests so that they can help localize the problem to the team that should be fixing the issue.

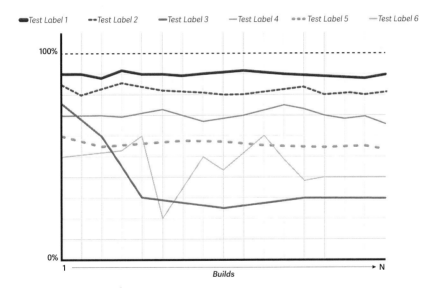

Figure 18: Environment Product Control Chart

With this graphic view of test passing rates or product control charts for a specific environment, we can quickly look across builds and see when new code came in that broke a significant number of tests. If these tests are labeled and grouped well, we can quickly identify the part of the system with the defect and have that team lead the triage. If we are running this test cycle daily, we only have to look at a limited number of change sets to triage the issue. This approach dramatically improves the productivity of the manual triage process. Having a graphic view of the same version of code running across different environments like shown in Figure 20 below will help us to quickly identify if it's the environment causing the issue.

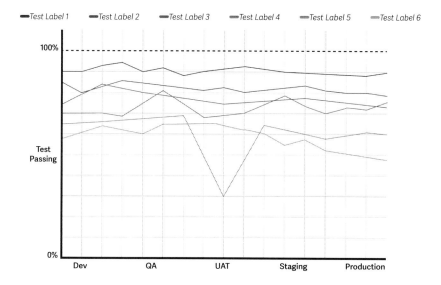

Figure 19: Product Control Chart Across Environments

If we are attempting to debug every test failure, we are going to get overwhelmed by the triage process. To be able to build in quality and fundamentally improve it over time, we need to develop product control charts with good graphical views and drilled down capabilities that make it easy and efficient to triage a large number of tests. These product control charts also help us understand the overall stability of the system which as we will show in chapter 7 can be used in combination with build acceptance tests to improve quality over time.

Application Driven Quality Expectations

The expectation that you have for quality for prerelease testing and how you build it in depends on the application and your ability to control deployment. It also depends on how the software is being used. For example, if it's for a medical device, your expectation of quality will be high and the software won't be updated very often. In this case, you will invest more in upfront testing. If it's for something like Facebook, where you have a small, loosely coupled team that runs its own deployment, you can do some testing up front and then use canary releases in production. This enables teams to move very quickly with limited risk. If you have a system where you don't control the deployment and/or have a large, tightly coupled system, you probably need to have higher quality expectations before releasing. Google's *Site Reliability Engineering: How Google Runs Productions Systems* did a good job of pointing out that there is a fundamental trade-off between the speed with which teams can move and quality expectations (Beyer et al. 2016, chap. 3). Part of the role of the operations, or site reliability engineering teams at Google, is to work with the development teams to set service level objectives. If the service level objective is 99% uptime, you can go at one rate of speed. If it is 99.999% uptime, then you need to slow down to ensure you are meeting the higher quality objectives. The reality is that for a given maturity of the deployment pipeline there is a real trade-off between speed and quality. This may seem counterintuitive based on some of the things that we're hearing coming out of the DevOps community, which has research that shows the best teams can deliver at high speeds with quality. In those cases, the teams' investment in their deployment pipelines enable them to go much faster and with higher quality than teams that don't have mature pipelines. They have also frequently decoupled their architecture so small teams can work independently. Those fundamental changes have enabled those teams to go faster with high quality. Those are important changes everyone should be implementing. At some point, however, you do reach a fundamental tradeoff between quality and speed given the capabilities of your deployment pipeline at any moment in time.

The quality expectations before release depend on the application and the ability to control deployment. If you have an application where you own the deployment, you can do canary releases and move very fast with limited risk. If you're creating embedded software for airplanes, the level of quality expectations you have before release are going to be fundamentally higher. When you look at quality for software, you need to look at your ability to control the deployment process, the expectations your customers have, and the impact of a quality problem.

At HP, we weren't able to control the deployment of firmware for the LaserJet Printers, and the customers weren't willing to update their firmware very frequently. We found that releasing more frequently than quarterly was a waste because none of our customers would update. We still tried to keep our code base fairly close to releasable every day. But with 10,000 hours of automated tests that we were running each day, we found the same tradeoff between quality and speed that Google highlights. We found that when we focused on driving the pass rate on those automated tests up to 98 or 99%, the throughput of features went down. Over time, we found that the right balance between speed and quality on a daily basis was closer to 90%. To optimize throughput of the organization, we kept the goal at 90% until we were getting ready for a quarterly release and then drove it to production level quality.

The quality and speed tradeoffs depends on the application and capabilities. Organizations that are used to one application and pipeline might not do a very good job of meeting quality expectations for different applications. I've seen examples where software development companies known for having industry leading DevOps capabilities for SaaS developed a poor-quality record once they had to start delivering components to embedded devices. Their culture was very focused on moving fast with the ability to rollback when there was a problem. When they lost that rollback capability and kept the culture of moving fast, they were delivering code quality that was unacceptable to their partners. How they delivered quality was really dependent on the application. When they controlled deployment, their fast-moving culture with the ability to respond was appropriate. When they move to embedded devices where they didn't control deployment, they needed to slow down and do much more rigorous pre-release testing because they lost the ability to respond quickly. The pre-release quality expectations for software depend on the application.

Changing the Process at the Rate of the Product

The additional challenge that software has is that every time you run the deployment pipeline, it's associated with a change to the product. With manufacturing, the challenge is keeping the process in control so you can build the same high-quality product. Once we've gotten the deployment pipeline stable, the biggest challenge for software is figuring out how we enable the process to change at the rate of the product. Containers are a really good example of where that's done from an environment perspective. Whenever developers need to change the environment, containers enable them to capture the environment change, encapsulate it with the code change, and couple that system together so that it all goes down the deployment pipeline as a unit. This is an example in software where we've enabled the product and the process to change at the same rate. Where we don't have containers in place, which is the case for a lot of different technologies, we're going to need to figure out how to make the environment and the product change at the same rate.

Test automation is another big challenge. I often talk about the page object model of test automation that Jeff Morgan created (Morgan 2017). I'm a real champion of that approach because it enables you to change the test automation at the same rate you are changing the product. But we haven't evolved to the point where it is easy to determine which tests have been affected by a code change. As an industry, we also haven't created a container-type solution for coupling the test and code changes together as a system. Similar challenges exist for database changes. There are tools out there like Liquid Base and Flyway that enable you to point to an environment and get it updated to a certain version of the database schema. But that doesn't mirror what we've done with containers. So, for the software industry there are still some innovations required to enable the process to easily change at the same rate as the product.

Summary

Software has a lot to learn from manufacturing about the advantages of building in quality versus inspecting it in later. It's going to require organizations to automate a lot of the repetitive tasks for consistency and then ensure they have a stable signal that they can use as quality feedback in the system. Once they have the new capability of the stable quality signal, they can start changing the rules to build in quality. This is probably one of the biggest changes you can make to improve the productivity of software development, but it isn't just a one-time thing. Once you get the quality signal stable, you need to be able to keep it stable by ensuring the process can change at the same rate as the product. Just like in manufacturing, building in quality is critical to improving productivity. It enables the next step of understanding and optimizing workflow, which we will cover in chapter 6.

CHAPTER 6

Understanding and Optimizing Workflow

In manufacturing, workflow is an observable process, and therefore it is easy to optimize and measure. You can count the number of products coming off the assembly line every month, week, day, hour, or minute. You know how much you are spending on manufacturing, so the key to improving productivity is optimizing the flow of the product through the entire factory. The same is not true for software. It is very hard to measure flow, because every product, feature, and story is a different size. It doesn't mean that the flow of value through the deployment pipeline isn't important—it's just that it is harder to focus on because it is so difficult to observe and measure.

The Theory of Constraints teaches us to improve flow by focusing on the constraint in the manufacturing process. Find the process with the slowest cycle time for a product or batch of products, and that is your constraint. With software, there is no natural constraint in the manufacturing process. The build, deploy, and test cycle can process 1 line of code change or 100,000 lines of code change in the same amount of time and for the same cost. This means that there is no bottleneck in the manufacturing process where inventory builds up. It also means that there are natural incentives to batch large amounts of inventory to process together. This overlooks the fact that there are bottlenecks in software outside the manufacturing process, such as those caused by manual triage and bug fixing, that are made much more difficult by these large batch sizes.

Optimizing flow for software requires understanding the constraints outside the manufacturing process and systematically addressing them. It requires an automated, stable quality signal we can use for building in quality as we discussed in Chapter 5. It requires eliminating manual quality gates that result in a buildup of inventory that has to be processed in large batch sizes that are hard to triage. Just because flow is hard to measure is no excuse for not systematically improving it. We need to be able to understand the issues that are slowing down flow in the deployment pipeline and systematically address them to the point where the constraint is on the developers. Then we need to do everything we can to help improve the productivity of the developers because that is constraining the flow of value through the organizations.

Manufacturing Approach to
Optimizing Workflow

Henry Ford found that if he focused on the flow of product through his factory with the assembly line, he could optimize and control the cost of his manufacturing process to make automobiles affordable for the masses. This works very well for a very high-volume manufacturing facility that is building one thing.

For other applications with more variability that weren't able to be linked together in a single piece assembly line, manufacturing thought leaders found that they needed different approaches for improvement. The first attempt used cost accounting to optimize the utilization of both equipment and people at every step. As Goldratt pointed out, though, this focus on cost accounting drove some very poor decisions (Goldratt and Cox 2004, chap. 4). For a manufacturing organization to be more effective, they need to be focused on the overall flow, the constraint in the system, and minimizing inventory. Goldratt used the Drum Buffer Rope approach to release work into production to minimize inventory. He also used his five focusing steps as a systematic approach for continuous improvement of the flow.

Everybody figured out in manufacturing that in order to improve flow and reduce the risk for quality problems, it was important to control the amount of excess inventory in the system. Henry Ford did that with a completely linked assembly line with very limited space for excess inventory. Goldratt did it with Drum Buffer Rope. Toyota did it using Kanban, which optimized Drum Buffer Rope further by holding a limited amount of inventory between each step in the manufacturing process.

The Toyota production system also created the Andon cord, which allowed anybody in the organization to pull the cord and stop the line when they saw a quality problem (Rother 2010, 100). It was important to stop the line because if they continued to run the process that was creating the product defects it would just keep building up defective inventory. These and other approaches are how manufacturing shifted to building in quality and optimizing workflow. It had dramatic impact on the quality of products and the efficiency of the organizations as they tried to improve the flow of product through their manufacturing lines.

Unique Characteristics and Capabilities of Software Related to Workflow

Physical products go through a development phase where you're trying to optimize the design of the product. Then they move to manufacturing where you're trying to optimize the flow and quality of the product. The real difference with software is that you're trying to do both manufacturing and development of the product at the same time. The process that you use for manufacturing software during development defines the flow of value through the organization, so it needs to be the focus of continuous improvement from the very beginning.

One of the biggest challenges with improving workflow is that it is hard to measure and see the flow with digital assets. Physical assets enable you to count the number of products created over time and see the inventory building up in the factory. Software flow is much harder to measure. In manufacturing, you create the same product over and over, so you want to measure if the changes to improve flow actually enabled you to create more products over a given amount of time. With software, the new features being added are different sizes every time, so it is much more difficult to see if changes improved the flow. Additionally, with software it's much harder to see the flow of value through the organization. You can't exactly walk out on the factory floor and see where inventory is building up in the system.

There is also no constraint in the software manufacturing process like there is in traditional physical products. If you're going to do a build, deploy, and test cycle, it takes the same amount of time and costs the same amount of money to do it for 1 line of code change as it does for 100,000 lines of code change. This is very different from manufacturing physical products where each cycle of the process only does one product or batch of products at a time. That's why they're so focused on the constraint in the manufacturing processes—inventory can back up in front of the process with the slowest cycle time. Software builds take all the inventory of new code that is checked in and runs it through the build, deploy, test cycle as a unit. Therefore, there is no bottleneck in the manufacturing process of software where inventory backs up and constrains the flow.

Because of the ability of the deployment pipeline to process 1 line of code or 100,000 lines of code for the same cost and cycle time, the natural tendency for software has been to batch up large amounts of inventory and send it through the process together. This overlooks one of the biggest bottlenecks that occurs in most organizations, which the manual process of triage and defect fixing. As you go to larger batch sizes, it makes triage much more inefficient because there are more potential sources of the defect that have to be evaluated.

With software, it's important to understand that we're looking for product defects that were created via manual coding as opposed to defects created by the automated process used to create physical products. Manufacturing pulls the Andon cord to stop the line and fix the process problem because if you let the process continue to run, you're going to create more defective product. With software, that's not the case because it is not the process that is creating the defects. What you need to do is stop the product defect from causing instability in the deployment pipeline and get it fixed as soon as possible. In software, what many people don't understand is that there is no need to stop the process because the process is not creating the defects. What you need to do is stop the product defect from impacting the deployment pipeline stability and get it fixed as quickly as possible. We do this with gating as discussed below. This is a concept many innovative thinkers don't get. Right now, the way they think about it in software has to do with red builds and stopping the line. I believe this is unnecessary. With gating, we can catch the defects without slowing down the flow for the code without defects.

Implications for Understanding and Optimizing Workflow for Software

Software needs to focus on improving flow as soon as product development starts because the flow defines the productivity of product development. Improving flow for software development depends on trying to understand the source of the constraint and how it moves over time as you make improvements. Software is unique in that it does not have constraints in the manufacturing process where inventory backs up. That is not to say that software development doesn't have bottlenecks. It is just to say that it doesn't exist in the manufacturing process. It is almost always in the manual tasks surrounding the manufacturing process. This can be in the manual execution of repetitive tasks. It can be in the triage and defect fixing process. It can be in the coding and creation of the product. It can be in coming up with ideas for new products or features. Or it can be in supporting the product in production.

Most organizations start with manual repetitive tasks as the bottleneck in the system, with testing being the most typical source. This manual testing can still process all the inventory waiting for each cycle, but it takes so long to do that it creates a bottleneck for most organizations that have not yet automated their testing. Once the repetitive tasks are automated, the next bottleneck tends to be the triage defect fixing process. This is why building in quality is so important. The goal of the organization is not triage and defect fixing. Rather, it is creating new products and features for the business. Therefore, time spent on triage and defect fixing is waste that should be reduced.

The ideal location for the bottleneck in software should be with the developers who are working with the business to deliver the value required. The work they are doing is the primary reason you are doing software development, so you want to be able to create as much of that value as possible. I've heard some people argue that the bottleneck should be in the ideation phase. Having been in a lot of large organizations for a long period of time, I will tell you that any organization that has the bottleneck in ideation for very long is probably going to end up right sizing their development organization. Having it in development is a more appropriate goal.

The bottleneck could also potentially be in operations if the development teams are going so fast that they are creating quality problems in production. Google SRE teams use service level objective agreements with development teams as a gate to ensure the bottleneck does not move to operations (Beyer et al. 2016, chap. 3). In this case, the development teams can move as fast as they want as long as the quality meets the service level objective.

Once the service level objective agreement is broken, development teams can't deploy any new features until the quality issues are addressed and the production is back under control. This is another form of a quality control gate that ensures the bottleneck doesn't move into operations.

Building in Quality to Improve Flow

One of the most important things that we can do to improve the flow for software is to automate all of the repetitive tasks. Being able to automatically build, create an environment, deploy, and test the latest code removes these repetitive tasks as a bottleneck. As we discussed in Chapter 5, this needs to be done in such a way that we have a stable quality signal that we can use to start building in quality. The automation of the deployment pipeline provides several significant advantages. First, automating these processes removes a fair amount of triage because the builds, deployments, environments, and tests are run the exact same way every time. Doing those steps manually results in errors that people make that need to be triaged and fixed. Second, automating the deployment pipeline makes smaller batch sizes that are easier to triage economically feasible. This is important because for most organizations once they start automating their deployment pipelines the bottleneck quickly moves to triage and defect fixing. Going to smaller batch sizes makes that triage more efficient.

The stable, quality signal with automation enables us to start building in quality, which helps reduce the waste associated with triage and defect fixing. Once we have the automated deployment pipeline in place, we're primarily looking for defects created by manual coding. We need to find the code that created the defect as quickly as possible and give that feedback to the developer so they can fix the issue. With small, loosely coupled teams, the new code can go from a developer's box to a test environment and into production using a canary release with very low risk. For those teams, that is the quickest way to get high quality feedback and ensure the developer knows the changes they need to make to build in quality.

For larger, tightly coupled systems and applications that don't own deployment, this process does not work as well. They need to make sure that they are integrating together large pieces of software to find quality issues. Doing that in production is not the most effective way. For these systems, as we build up our different subsystems and assemblies in the deployment pipeline, we need to make sure that we're finding those product defects as close to the source as possible and ensuring they don't impact stability. We don't need to do this by stopping line like we do in manufacturing because it's not the process that is creating the product defects. It is the manual code that is creating them. We want to give that feedback to the developer as quickly as possible and ensure the defect doesn't impact the rest of the deployment pipeline.

Creating gates to build in quality does this. The most common form is gated commits. With this process, every time a developer tries to commit code to trunk it kicks off a set of automated build acceptance tests. If the tests pass, then the code makes it to trunk and is ready for the next stage of the deployment pipeline. If it doesn't, the build fails, and the code is sent back to the developer to fix the defect and build in the right amount of quality as shown in Figure 20 below.

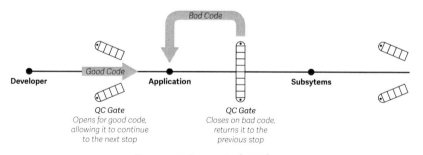

Figure 20: Gating Code Defects

In manufacturing, we stop the line to keep the process from creating more defects. In software, we are able to keep the line flowing and send the defective code back to the developer to get fixed. Software has this unique capability of allowing us to catch the product defect and send it back to the individual, all while enabling flow of good code to keep moving through the organization. We don't need to pull the Andon cord to stop the line. But we do need to make sure that the product defects don't make it into the broader system. We can gate quality at the application. We can gate at the subsystem. We can gate this as a larger system as it goes into production as shown in Figure 21 below.

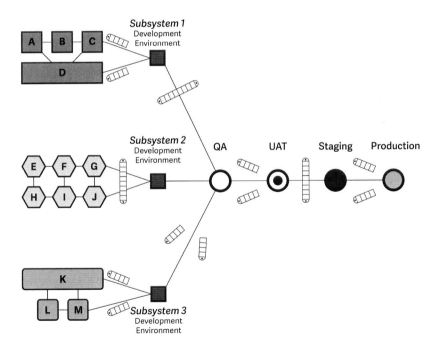

Figure 21: Gating code defects across the Deployment Pipeline

In large organizations with tightly coupled systems, this is a fundamental breakthrough. This is how we build in quality at the same time as optimizing flow through the entire system. The goal of the design for the deployment pipeline with gating is to enable us to localize the triage as much as possible. We want to find defects in the deployment pipeline as close to the source as we can because there are fewer changes that have to be evaluated in triage. There are also fewer people impacted by the instability of the defect. The further right a defect goes into the system, the more people that have code in that environment and are impacted by the instability.

Our goal with the deployment pipeline is to find as many of the product defects as close to the sources as possible and keep the integrated test environments that are further to the right as stable as possible. This is accomplished using quality gates to capture the defects. Once these baseline quality gates are in place, you can start increasing the stability of the deployment pipeline by adding more and more tests to the gates.

Eliminating Manual Quality Gates to Improve Workflow

One of the biggest mistakes that a lot of software organizations make is using manual testing to gate code through different stages of the deployment pipeline. They do this because they know manual testing can find things that automation can't. A lot of organizations don't have all the automation in place, so they use manual testing to keep defects from making it further down the deployment pipeline. These are all good intentions, but they overlook the fact that the time lag associated with manual testing causes large batches of inventory that make the triage process more inefficient and delays finding defects associated with interaction between different components.

Because of that, most DevOps organizations would recommend automating everything and getting rid of any manual testing. But this overlooks the fact that manual testing is better at finding certain types of issues. The right balance is to use manual testing where required. For example, UAT testing, exploratory, and usability can still be manual. Manual testing just shouldn't be used for gating. Instead, make sure that you're allowing all the code to flow as quickly through the system as you possibly can and use automated testing gates to drive the quality as high as possible. This provides a stable environment that has all the latest code that can be used for manual testing on a daily basis. Manual testing can always be run in these environments because the gates ensure they are stable. When manual testers find issues, they can enter a defect, but they shouldn't be waiting till the end of development to start testing and using the manual testing as a gate.

Automate the processes in the deployment pipeline to speed the flow as much as possible. Define the quality signal so it can capture and send back the defective product code as quick as possible and limit it from impacting the stability of the deployment pipeline.

Making the Flow Visible

Finding the balance between flow and building in quality is key to optimizing the deployment pipeline. Providing visibility of digital factories is the first step. In Chapter 4, we took our architecture and broke it down into the deployment pipeline to make that visible. We further increased the visibility in Chapter 5 with quality control charts. Now we need to ensure we are making issues associated with the flow of our digital assets visible.

First, we need to understand how long it takes for value to flow through the system. We need to create visibility for how long does it take from code being checked in to being available to the customer. Next, we need to know where our defects are being found in the deployment pipeline. Our goal is to find the defects as soon after we have an individual writing code as possible so that they're still thinking about the code. They can learn from the experience while the code is still fresh in their minds instead of beating them up for something they don't even remember. Therefore, we need to make sure we're tagging the defects that get entered in the system and where they get found on the deployment pipelines so we can look at the delay in that feedback. Figure 22 on page 90 uses defect tagging and the deployment pipeline to show cycle time and the feedback delay.

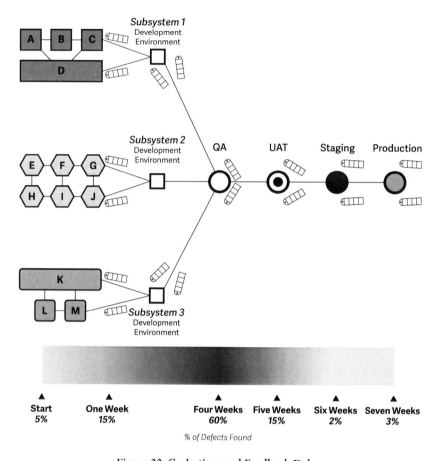

Figure 22: Cycle-time and Feedback Delay

This example shows that 60% of the defects are found 4 weeks after the developer are writing code which is too slow to help them improve.

Visibility of the inventory in the system is also important. In manufacturing, whether it was Henry Ford or Goldratt or Toyota, the focus is on minimizing inventory in the system because it impacts flow and quality. Minimizing inventory in the system has the same impact on software but because the inventory is digital it isn't very visible. We change this by improving the visibility of inventory that exists in the system. We need to understand how much work is at risk of unknown quality problems because it has not been integrated together.

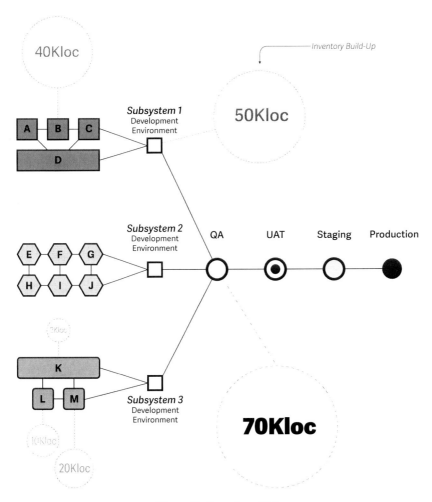

Figure 23: Inventory Risk

Currently, that inventory is not very visible to most organizations. We need to make that inventory visible by mapping the lines of code at each stage of the deployment pipeline that haven't been integrated into the next stage with graphics like Figure 23 above. This shows the inventory risk that is building up in the system.

Optimizing Development Work

The goal in optimizing the flow for software development is to move the bottleneck to the developer and then, as Goldratt taught us, to optimize the productivity of the developers to improve flow even more. Exploiting the system constraint requires understanding everything that is slowing down developers and working to remove those issues over time.

One of the most common things that impacts developers is handoffs between different teams. They end up getting slowed down waiting for responses from others. To reduce this issue organizations go to whole teams that can address any issue. This is the DevOps idea that the team owns everything from the business idea to production. This is ideal for small teams that can work independently. It doesn't work as well in large, tightly coupled systems where there are frequently more specialists. In these larger organizations where we have common resources that are supporting different development teams, we need to ensure these common resources are not slowing down the teams. This requires these common resources to have excess capacity, and as Donald Reinertsen taught us in *The Principles Product Development Flow*, we need to measure these common resources on responsiveness instead of utilization (Reinertsen 2009, chap. 7).

We can improve the effectiveness of the triage and defect fixing process for developers by providing high quality feedback from our quality gates. This feedback should include any logging from the test failure, ideally scrubbed back to what matters most. It should include the ability to easily rerun the test on the developer's desktop and anything else than can improve productivity.

We can also help developers understand how to improve before they even check in with code reviews. This is probably the best and highest quality feedback that can help improve manual work. Similar to the apprentice days of manual manufacturing, one of the best ways to learn how to do the job better is by learning from someone that has been making mistakes longer. The code reviews can be done with someone who has more experience with new architectures, like Pat in the LaserJet example. Or they can be done with someone who has a fresh set of eyes that can catch anything you've missed before it gets into the larger system and becomes harder to triage.

As we automated the deployment pipeline at HP, we realized the constraint had moved to the developers. The flow was properly constrained by them, so we did everything we could think of to make them more productive. We provided all the developers with noise cancellation headphones because we knew it can be hard to focus on coding in large shared work environments. We provided developers with extra-large monitors because we understood that being able to easily see more of the code at one time helped them be more productive.

Technology has also had a big impact on developer productivity. The software industry is constantly changing the languages it uses. This isn't done on a whim, but because it is understood that it can have a dramatic impact on developer productivity. Very few people write compilers any more, they just use them. Additionally, very few people have to write libraries because there is typically one around that will meet their requirements. This ability to leverage work from others to enable focus on the unique business value being added is key to making developers more productive. Cornelia Davis at Pivotal Labs gave a great presentation at DOES18 in Las Vegas on how new languages can have a significant impact on developer productivity and debug (Davis 2018). This might not be the right answer for everyone but it helps reinforce the point that we need to be constantly focused on finding new languages, tools, and processes to help improve developer productivity.

Summary

The focus on flow during software development is important because it drives the productivity of the organization. We can use Goldratt's Theory of Constraints as a systematic approach to improving flow, but we need to understand that software is unique in that it is hard to measure flow. And there is not a natural constraint in the software manufacturing process.

Automating the deployment pipeline and getting a stable signal provides breakthrough capabilities that you can use to improve flow and build in quality. It enables the gating of product defects with automated testing. We can still use manual testing where appropriate, but we don't want it to slow down the flow and build up inventory that is at risk of rework.

As we improve the deployment pipeline, the constraint in the system is going to change and ideally land on developers. As it does, we need to do everything possible to help improve their productivity because that defines the rate at which we can deliver value through the system.

So far, we have laid the foundation for product design/development, building in quality, and focusing on flow. Next, we will look at how to continually improve each of these aspects of software development.

CHAPTER 7

Continuous Improvement

The manufacturing industry has a long history of continuous improvement, starting with Fredrick Winslow Taylor. They are constantly working to improve quality and workflow in their organizations. In fact, Toyota will let competitors see how they run their factories because they don't believe how they are running them today is their competitive advantage (Rother 2010, chap. 1). They feel their true competitive advantage is the Kata process or their culture of continuous improvement. Competitors can learn by seeing how they run their factories, but by the time they implement those changes, Toyota will be so far ahead due to the Kata process that what their competitors learned won't make a big difference.

Most software organizations today don't have that same cultural focus on continuous improvement. They are so focused on delivering the next set of features that even when waste or technical debt is identified, nobody is provided time to fix the issues. This is partly due to the fact that in software we look at it through the lens of product development instead of thinking about how we manufacture the software during development. In manufacturing, those are two different phases with two different organizations. One group figures out how to design the best product. The other group is focused on continuous improvement of quality and flow in production. In software, we don't have a separate group focused on continuous improvement. We have one team that needs to do both at the same time.

Unlike manufacturing, software is very flexible, so the product can be continually improved to help better meet its business intent and to make the deployment pipeline more efficient. This chapter will look at what we can learn from the deep history of continuous improvement in manufacturing and show how to modify those approaches for software.

We laid the foundations for this chapter in the last three chapters. We will start by looking at culture because there is a big opportunity for improvement in this area. Next, we will look at product development and design. Software is very unique in that the product can continually be improved. We will show how software can leverage the A3 process for product improvement to create a more systematic approach to achieving the business intent. Next, we will review how the architecture can be modified over time to continually improve the efficiency of the deployment pipeline all the way through deployment. These architectural improvements will be focused on the principle of improving flow, but the practices will need to be fine-tuned to address all the different types of applications and deployment pipelines defined in Chapter 4. Next, we review how to continually improve quality over time based on the foundation we established in Chapter 5. Finally, we will review how to continually improve flow through the organization.

The goal of this chapter is to show in more detail all the different things you can and should be continually improving in software development. In Chapter 9, we will develop a more systematic approach for prioritizing these different types of improvements.

Manufacturing Approach to Continuous Improvement

Frederick Winslow Taylor started continuous improvement in manufacturing with his time and motion studies (Wikipedia 2019,

"Frederick Winslow Taylor"). This worked well when the manufacturing activities were very manual and dependent on how each individual was doing tasks. He would time how long it took different workers to complete a task and then try to figure out the most efficient method of doing that specific task. This would become the best practice, and he would work to have everybody in the organization do things in that exact same, most efficient, way.

As things became more automated and complex in manufacturing, there needed to be a better method for improvement. Because the process and automation were creating the product, the best way to improve the effectiveness was to focus on process improvement by analyzing how the product moved through the different manufacturing steps with value stream analysis and improving each step along the process using the scientific method. Taiichi Ohno created this methodology at Toyota because he realized that if he was going to be able to compete with high volume car manufacturers in the United States, he was going to have to be able to improve at a rate that was faster than anybody else. He came up with the Toyota Kata process, which leveraged the scientific method to continually improve every aspect of manufacturing.

He didn't make the same mistakes that Taylor did by figuring out the best way and then telling people how to do it. He realized that there were a couple of very important steps involved in making this change happen. The first step was finding the best ideas and most efficient means of manufacturing. The second step was getting the workers to embrace the new approach. This required including everyone in the process so that they would be personally invested in the improvements. Therefore, with the Kata process it was not just the industrial engineers figuring out the best way. He engaged the entire organization in the continuous improvement journey. As a Toyota employee, you didn't just do the job, you were also responsible for figuring out how that job could be done better.

When you're looking at changing how an organization works, if you can include the people who actually have to implement the process, you are going to have less resistance to change. Nobody likes to change how they have been working for years, and if you just tell them they have to do it this way now, there is going to be even more resistance. Instead, if you get them engaged in solving a problem, not only will they try to find the best ways to do that, but they'll also take ownership for making their ideas successful. The Toyota Kata approach was to engage the entire organization in continuous improvement. The manager's job was to help teach a systematic approach to problem solving using the scientific method. It was then everyone's job to use this approach to continually improve. This Toyota Kata process is captured in the Lean Six Sigma approach, which is a very systematic approach to continuous improvement that is used across manufacturing.

Goldratt took this a step further by helping us focus our improvement efforts on the bottleneck because any change made outside of the constraint wasn't going to improve the flow of the factory. He used his five focusing steps to enable us to understand how to locate and improve the constraint. This systematic approach to improving flow is ingrained in most successful manufacturing organizations today.

Unique Characteristics and Capabilities of Software Related to Continuous Improvement?

Software is very unique in that the product can and should be continually improved. This is really important because software improvements frequently don't get used or have the desired impact. The best way to find more things that the customer will use and to meet the business's intent is to release small changes frequently and look for the customer's feedback.

Another thing that is unique about software is that how we manufacture it (our deployment pipeline) defines the productivity of software development. Because it's cheap and easy to create, you can start with the very first line of code. For software, we're trying to make sure that we bring up the deployment pipeline from the first line of code and then continually improve it until we quit improving the product.

One more thing that is unique about software is the lack of focus on continuous improvement. Most organizations don't really think closely about how value flows through their organization. They're very focused on the product meeting schedules and commitments to specifications. They're measuring their software organizations based on the accuracy of the plan, which is a very product development-focused perspective. In contrast, a manufacturing-focused perspective emphasizes how value flows. As somebody who spent a lot of my career doing continuous improvement in manufacturing, when I moved over to software, the lack of focus on continuous improvement both for the product and the process really struck me.

With software, architecture or product design has a big impact on the efficiencies. There are things that we can continually change about the architecture that will enable a different design of the deployment pipeline and more efficient flow. Because of that, we should be evolving our product architecture over time, not just for how it's used by the customer but for how value can flow through the organization.

Software flow is very hard to measure. Manufacturing can measure the number of products going down the line. That is hard with software because the size of each feature is different, which makes it very difficult to have a quantifiable measure of flow.

Implications for Continuous Improvement of Software

Software is so flexible that there is a broad range of product design and process implementations that can be continually improved. The biggest change for the industry is to create a culture of continuous improvement. This is a big focus for any manufacturing organization once the product is released. The problem with software is that the same organization is doing both product development and continuous improvement, so it is hard to achieve the same level of focus. That needs to change if software is going to see the same level of improvements as manufacturing has experienced.

Software also needs to realize that both the product and the process should be a focus of continuous improvement. The product improvement should be focused on ensuring that customers are using the changes and that those changes are also meeting the business intent. The product architecture should also be modified to improve the efficiencies of the deployment pipeline by focusing on the principle of flow. The type of architectural changes required will depend on the specific application. The architectural improvement section will review each of the different types of applications described in Chapter 4 and the types of improvements that will improve the efficiencies of each type of application and deployment pipeline. We will review changes that will help improve deployments for applications that don't directly control deployments so they can improve flow of value all the way to the end user.

In Chapter 5, we talked about how to build in quality, but this is not a one-time thing. Here we will review how, once we have a stable quality signal, we can start improving our ability to build in quality over time. In Chapter 6, we reviewed how improving flow is difficult with software because the flow is so hard to measure. In this chapter we review how to improve flow by focusing on waste that is providing resistance to flow. While it is hard to measure flow, it is not that hard to measure waste. In this chapter, we will review all the metrics that can be used to measure waste as a method of prioritizing changes for improving flow.

Creating a Culture of Continuous Improvement

The focus on continuous improvement is probably the biggest thing we can learn from manufacturing. It's not just finding the one best way like Taylor did. What we really need to do is figure out how to engage the entire organization to continually improve both the product and the process. This expectation needs to start at the top, and it needs to involve a systematic approach. Everyone should be expected to not just do their job, but also be thinking about how to improve how the job is done. They need to be given the time to implement the improvements. There also needs to be a systematic approach for identifying the best opportunities for improvement and measuring the impact of the changes.

This is probably one of the biggest challenges for software. Most organizations are so busy cutting with the saw focused on delivering business value that they don't take the time to sharpen the saw so they can deliver even more business value. This is going to have to change for software before it will see the kind of dramatic improvements manufacturing achieved with a systematic approach. Ideally, this will need to start at the top. We will cover this in more detail with the different executives' roles in Chapter 9, "Systematic Approaches for Software Improvement."

Product Continuous Improvement

If we're going to get the entire organization focused on product improvement, we need to be really clear about how we measure if the product is meeting its business intent. In their book *Lean Enterprise: How High Performance Organizations Innovate at Scale*, Jez Humble, Joanne Molesky, and Barry O'Reilly discuss the need for software to be focused on continuous improvement of the product and the fact that we should use the scientific method each time we come up with an idea to improve (2015). We need to create a hypothesis about what we thought it would improve, make the change, and measure the impact of the improvement. Even though this book came out in 2015, I still go into very few organizations that are measuring their product and have clear metrics in place.

To address the lack of a systematic approach to product improvement, we should take advantage of some of the structure that Taiichi Ohno put in place at Toyota, such as the A3 process for doing continuous process improvement. Software development should develop a similar A3 process for doing product improvement. The A3 chart typically has the planning or problem definition on the left side of the chart and the implementation and validation on the right side of the chart. The first step is defining metrics that capture the business intent of the product. If we are trying to improve the navigation component for a website, we need to measure how well individuals are finding what they need. How many searches result in a customer adding a product to their shopping cart? How many of the searches end up with a purchase? If we are working on a social media application, we should measure how many people share posts and how many more people view them. These metrics are specific to the application, but if we want people to continually improve the product, we need to be able to measure the business intent we are trying to achieve. These metrics need to be fine-tuned by business leaders for the applications and made visible to the organization through the A3 process if you are going to successfully engage everyone in the continuous improvement process.

The A3 chart should also have a section to list the backlog of new features or hypotheses to be tested next. This is the list of changes that are most likely to improve the business intent metrics. The implementation side of the A3 chart should also include the features currently under development. The other challenge with software is that a large proportion of features we develop are not even used. To continually improve the product, we should have good metrics on the usage rates for each of the features.

We also want to ensure the product is not overly improved. Organizations get so focused on coming up with new ideas that they tend to over-deliver features, which can also mean those features end up not being used. It's important when we're looking at product continuous improvement to try to quantify when we've reached the point when we're over-delivering features. To do this, it's important to look at how much we are spending on product development versus how good a job we are doing at moving the metrics that define the business intent. When we start reaching a point of diminishing returns, we most likely need to take a different approach or look at moving people to an application with more opportunities to impact the business. Therefore, the A3 chart should include a time-based graph showing the impact of releases on the business metrics. Figure 24 below is an example of how to apply the A3 process improvement rigor to continuous improvement of the product in software.

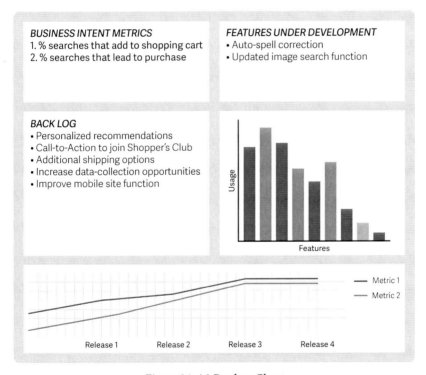

Figure 24: A3 Product Chart

Architectural Continuous Improvement

Just like with DFX in manufacturing, how the product is architected has broad implications not only for how it is used, but also for the lifetime costs of developing and supporting it. The product design can be improved to make it easier to test.

The architecture also impacts the design and efficiency of the deployment pipeline. The type of changes required to improve the flow are very application dependent. In the next several sections, we will look at the different types of continuous improvement changes we can make to the architecture to simplify the deployment pipeline and make it more efficient. The principles will focus on design changes to improve flow, but the types of improvements required will be very dependent on the application. Therefore, we will review the architectural changes that are most important for each type of application and deployment pipeline discussed in Chapter 4.

API Testing

How you design the business logic within the UI can have a very significant effect on how you're able to do testing. The more the business logic is tied up in the UI, the more automated UI testing is required. This automated UI testing is harder to maintain, slower, and tends to be more brittle. You can improve the quality of those tests over time, but you can probably get much more significant improvements if you move to API testing by removing the business logic from the UI. That is one continuous improvement approach that you can use with the architecture to make the organization more effective. The other is to really look at the impact of the product design on the deployment pipeline in the architecture.

Loosely Coupled Systems

The easiest and most efficient deployment pipeline is where we have loosely coupled architecture that enables small teams to work independently, which enables them to move fast and get rapid feedback from customers with approaches like canary releases. If you are lucky enough to be working on this type of architecture, you don't need architectural changes to improve the deployment pipeline. Your bottleneck is probably somewhere else.

Tightly Coupled Systems

If you have a large, tightly coupled system requiring many parts of your organization to work together, you can become more efficient by breaking those couplings so teams can work independently. Currently, the most popular approach in the industry is moving to micro-services. These micro-services include the UI, the business logic, the services, and the database all encapsulated together. They have good testing interfaces around them that enable those teams to independently develop, qualify, and deploy code.

There are two fundamental approaches you can use when you have a large, tightly coupled system and you want to have more independence between teams so you can move faster. One is to spin off a bunch of small micro-services over time to loosely couple the system. The other approach is to take your large, tightly coupled system and look at places where you can break it into subsystems. See if you can create decoupling at those interfaces and enforce it with automated testing. Instead of having a thousand different people working on the application, you can have three teams of 300 people. Then, over time, you can break each team of 300 into three teams of 100 and use that process to decouple your monolith. When you use this approach, it is important that you're also decoupling the database. If you don't take away that coupling, you're going to have a hard time separating your deployment pipeline and getting smaller teams to run independently.

If you have a large, tightly coupled system, you should really look at decoupling it so that the smaller teams can work more independently and move faster. This can be done with micro-services or decoupling into subsystems. Micro-services are probably the ideal design, but it can take a while before there are enough micro-services to decouple the monolith. These micro-services also increase the complexity for operations. Decoupling into smaller subsystems provides more immediate benefits and is easy for operations, but it is a slower path to the ideal design.

Think about the problem you are trying to address and the quickest way to get there for your specific application.

Customized Off-the-Shelf Software

If you develop large applications that customers deploy and customize on their site, then you have different opportunities for improving the architecture. In this case, one of your biggest challenges is the number of different branches that you have to support to deal with the customer's unwillingness to upgrade to the latest version. There are a couple of reasons customers don't like to upgrade that need to be addressed. First, upgrading versions is a lot of work. Second, there are frequently quality issues with the upgrade because they are using the product in a way that you are not testing.

The architecture can be improved to make it easier to upgrade. Create APIs in the architecture between the customizations and the application. Work to get that interface stable over time with automated test. You want customers to be able to capture all the customizations in a source code management (SCM) tool and automatically apply them on top of the application. Provide a framework that customers can use to create stable automated tests. These changes in the product design make it much easier for customers to upgrade. They can take the latest upgrade from the provider, automatically apply a known good version of the customizations, and run their automated tests to ensure it is still working. If it is not, they know the problem is due to the new version of code. They can also take a known good version of the application, modify the customizations in the SCM, automatically apply the changes, and then test. If they have a problem, they know it is due to the changes in the customization. They can then review the changes documented in the SCM to quickly triage the issue. Changing the product design in these ways enables changes in the deployment pipeline, which enable more efficient triage and improves flow.

The other reason why customers tend not to upgrade is they find quality issues that require working with the vendor to provide patches. This lack of quality makes the customers reluctant to upgrade, and they often prefer to just get patches on their current version. Providers are going to need to address the quality issues if they are ever going to get away from the inefficiencies of having to support so many different branches. This will require building in quality. Moving to a clean API with automated testing should help a lot, but providers that have ongoing quality issues in the field need to ensure the problematic customizations are built into the quality gates in their deployment pipeline.

Sharing development costs of common applications across lots of companies by having a vendor provide a common application that can be customized makes sense as an approach. The challenge is that the product design of most of these applications makes it very inefficient for both the provider and the user. The architecture of the products should be continually improved so it is easier for the customer to have all the newest improvements and the provider can eliminate the inefficiencies of having to support multiple branches.

Embedded Software

One of the biggest sources of inefficiency for embedded products is the duplication of testing, triage, and defect fixing that occurs further right on the deployment pipeline as shown in Figure 25 on page 108. The further to the right, the more you have to test and triage on multiple versions of the configuration. The code that can be tested on a simulator can typically be tested, triaged, and fixed once and then used on all the different products. It is also typically very efficient because this testing can occur automatically on virtual machines in a server farm that is relatively cheap. At HP, we were running around 10,000 hours of automated simulator testing a day on 10 million lines of code running in four racks of servers. This was a big enabler of our productivity breakthroughs.

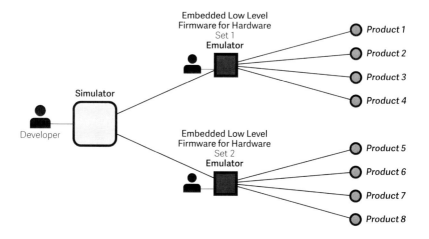

Figure 25: Embedded Deployment Pipeline

The next best place to test is on emulators that include the custom hardware for the product. These are typically harder to get and more expensive than simulators because the custom hardware is expensive and in short supply early in the product development lifecycle. The number of different versions that need to be tested depends on the amount of hardware variation. At HP, we were supporting both MIPS and ARM based processsors, so we always had at least two different versions of emulators. Early on at HP, each product team was also developing a custom imaging processor that required the firmware to support more hardware variations. As the cost of developing these custom chips went up and the cost of the chips themselves went down, it no longer made as much sense to have as many different versions of custom hardware. This reduction in hardware variability resulted in a simpler deployment pipeline with fewer different types of emulators.

The reduction in hardware variability can improve the efficiency of developing software and firmware for embedded devices. This goes against the natural reaction of most product organizations. They have been competing based on product cost for so long that their natural reaction is to be constantly changing the hardware to save the next penny. This worked fine when they were competing based on cost, but that is starting to change as more of the products are differentiated based on the software that is running on top of the hardware. In these cases, hardware variability driven by cost reductions can dramatically increase the cost of software development and slow down their ability to compete based on software. One of the biggest challenges for products with embedded software and firmware is to find the right balance between product cost reduction and the efficiencies of their deployment pipeline. This is a huge cultural shift for most product organizations.

The most inefficient place for testing is on the actual product. This is the point on the deployment pipeline that has the most variation because testing has to be duplicated on each product. It is also the hardest place to automate testing. While you may need to do some final validation on the product, you should always be striving to build in quality upstream where it is more efficient.

There are architectural changes embedded organizations can make to improve the efficiencies of their deployment pipeline. There is software code that can be efficiently developed on a simulator. There's code that really touches the custom hardware that must be developed and qualified on an emulator. There are things that need to be tested on the final product. What we're trying to do with embedded software as shown in Figure 26 on page 110 is to move as much of the code base up into the simulator space as possible. This requires a very solid hardware abstraction layer between the low-level firmware and the code that we can treat more like software. Over time, we want to move more and more of the code up above that hardware obstruction layer to take advantage of the benefits simulator-based development provides. We need to ensure that hardware differences are handled below the hardware abstraction layer so we don't find new software issues as we do testing on emulators and the final product.

Ideally, you want to be able to find as many of the defects in your software code as possible on the simulator. This is going to

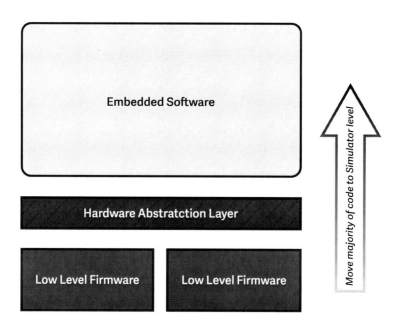

Figure 26: Architectural Improvements for Embedded Systems

require investing and improving your simulator overtime. The next best place is to find defects on the emulators with the custom hardware. You want to try to avoid finding defects here because it's more expensive and it's hard to afford as many emulators as simulators. The worst place to find them is on the product. Ideally, you want to architect the product and improve your simulator and emulator to find as many defects as possible before product testing. Because as you're going down your deployment pipeline, the testing, triage, and defect fixing gets distributed across different test environments, and you lose the advantage of being able to develop, test, and qualify the code once and use it as many places as required. As shown in Figure 27 on page 111 with software, we're trying to aggregate that work at a common place. If we can pull back testing and finding defects further to the left in the deployment pipeline, it is more efficient. This requires improvement in the architecture, reduction in hardware variability, and investments in simulators and emulators.

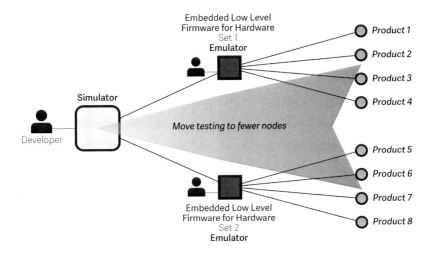

Figure 27: Improving Embedded Deployment Pipelines

Deployment

Deployment can be the biggest bottleneck to flow for organizations that do not control when their code is updated. It's important to realize that customers may not want to update their firmware or product software as frequently as you'd like and that you will have to deal with those implications. If you've got a point of sale type of application where you have thousands of different end users, you're not going to want to be changing that UI on a very frequent basis. You want to avoid making it confusing and difficult for them to use the product because they have to be constantly training on the new capabilities. There are changes behind the scenes that you can make without impacting them that may not be as big of a deal, but constant changes to their interface might be a problem.

There are organizations that have struggled with these problems and found different solutions. At HP, we ended up only releasing quarterly because we couldn't get our customers to upgrade their firmware on a more frequent basis. In your daily life, you have likely experienced different organizations addressing this challenge and increasing flow. One example is on your phone. It used to be that you had to accept upgrades to applications. Now the updates to applications are automatically done behind the scenes so the software is being upgraded on a more frequent basis. When it comes to updates to the operating system, you still have to approve it, but they now constantly remind you that you need to upgrade until you accept.

Traditional automobile companies understand that people aren't going to update their software or firmware in the field. Tesla has taken a fundamentally different approach because they understand that digital is how they compete. The quicker they can rollout value and get feedback from customers, the more effective they are going to be as a digital organization. As a result, with Tesla you're able to upgrade your firmware on an ongoing basis in your garage.

There are things that can and should be done to improve the frequency of deployment even if you don't have complete control. This should be part of the focus on continuous improvement of flow if deployment is a major bottleneck. The approach needs to be cognizant of the impacts on customers because the goal is to increase the flow of value without causing too much disruption.

Improving Software Quality

Software quality can and should be being continually improved. The quality chapter discussed the importance and steps required to ensure a stable quality signal. The workflow chapter covered how to build in quality by gating code based on automated tests. From a continuous improvement perspective, we want to start improving the quality that we're building into the product at a rate that the developers can handle. They need to get good at bringing in changes without breaking existing functionality. At the start, you don't need to have a lot of tests to start seeing improvements. In fact, when you start with too many tests, it becomes much too difficult to get their code through the quality gates, and the developers just get frustrated. It's more important to start with a few good tests and have the developers learn how to make it through the quality gates. The best way to figure out which test to start with is to go to your manual testers and ask what types of things they frequently see in this application that make it not very useful to test. Start with those tests. With as few as five automated tests, you can start to build in quality and immediately make your manual testers more productive because they will be working in more stable environments. Over time, as you get good at keeping those build acceptance test passing, go back to the manual testers to figure out the next set of automated tests they would like to see added to the gating. Work with them to write those automated tests and add them to the build acceptance test. Use this process over time to continually improve the quality of your gates.

Product control charts are the other source of new tests to add to gating. The build acceptance tests are a limited set that needs to run fast enough to support the small batch sizes that are required for efficient triage. As you create more automated testing for better coverage, you realize it takes too long to run every test on every build. Therefore, each day take the latest green build from the day and run a full set of automated regression tests. Plot the passing rates for the different test labels over time. This is your product control chart. Use these charts to find holes in the build acceptance tests. Look at your product control charts over time to see where defects are making it through your build acceptance tests and having a dramatic impact on passing rates. For example, in Figure 28 on page 114 you can see that test passing rate for label 6 dropped significantly between build number 5 and build number 6. When you see significant drops in passing rates, fix the defect, then add a test that caught the defect to the build acceptance tests. When you have a large number of automated tests running frequently, you can't afford to debug every failure. Instead you need to use the product control charts to statistically improve quality. Build acceptance tests with gating is the most valuable tool because it builds in quality without the overhead of having to log, track, and close defects. The product control charts find holes in the build acceptance tests. Continuous improvement of quality requires constantly optimizing the build acceptance tests. This requires removing build acceptance tests that aren't finding defects and using the product control charts to identify tests that should be added. This is how you continually improve quality over time.

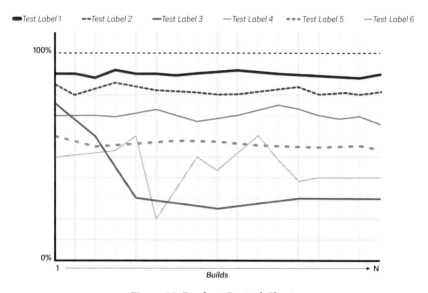

Figure 28: Product Control Chart

This approach should be used at each quality gate on the deployment pipeline. Look for defects that are found later in the pipeline and work to find ways to optimize the tests that gate the code, applications, or subsystems to ensure the issues are caught earlier. This makes triage easier because there are fewer changes to evaluate at the source of the problem. It blocks the defect from moving further down the deployment pipeline and causing instability that impacts more people. The quality of the automated gates needs to improve to the point that manual testing can be removed as a quality gate. The manual testing can still occur, but it should be done on a more frequent basis in the new, more stable environment to the right of the deployment pipeline. These are the types of approaches that continually improve how you build quality into your software applications, which enables much quicker flow of value through your organization.

Improving Software Flow

Moving into software from manufacturing, I came to the conclusion that you can't manage software with metrics the way that you can in manufacturing. In software, my opinion was "Tell me how you're going to measure me, and I'll tell you how I'm going to behave." If you want to measure me in terms of productivity on lines of code of changes, I can copy and paste better than anybody. How many lines do I need to complete to show the productivity improvement that you're looking for to show the improvement of flow through the organization? Instead of writing code efficiently with objects that are leveraged, I can copy and paste the code into a bunch of different places to meet the metric that you're trying to achieve and make the application very hard to maintain.

If you'd rather measure me based on feature throughput, I can play that game too. I used to go to the bathroom as a feature, but now that I need more features points, I break that into smaller stories to show that I'm improving my productivity. I walk down the hall. I go to the bathroom. I open the door. I go into the bathroom. I come back. How many features points did you say I needed to show the productivity gain that you're trying to achieve? For that reason, I've been coaching executives that it's really important to go out in the organization and get a qualitative feel for what is getting in the way of your organization being productive so that you can prioritize improvements to address those inefficiencies. That is what I did as a leader, so I assumed that is what they should be doing.

What I've realized as I've consulted with more and more organizations is that it's hard to get executives to spend the time necessary to get that qualitative feel. I've also seen what organizations can accomplish by putting good metrics in place to drive behaviors across very large organizations. Over time, I've started to see the value of having good metrics within the software that you can use to drive behavior changes. I still don't believe that we can do a very good job of measuring flow of value through the organization or productivity because each feature, each product, each new capability is a very different size. But as I have been spending time going into organizations and helping them improve, I've realized that I have gotten very good at measuring the waste and inefficiency in organizations. Where we can't measure the flow of value, we can measure the waste that is slowing down flow to prioritize improvements. We can also measure if our improvements are reducing that waste. Instead of measuring our ability to improve flow like is done in manufacturing, in software we need to measure our ability to remove waste that is slowing down the flow. The following subsections review the metrics for different types of waste that are slowing down flow. Improving flow requires reviewing these metrics for the deployment pipeline to determine the biggest source of waste that is slowing down flow, then systematically addressing all the sources of waste from biggest to smallest until the bottleneck is on the developers.

Cycle Time and Feedback Delays

Looking at flow for the organization, it's important to be able to understand the cycle time that it takes from when a developer checks in code to when it's ready to release to the customer. When I first started working with organizations, my perspective was that cycle time was defined by how long it took to test, how long it took to deploy, how long it took to create an environment, and how long it took to move code through that process. What surprised me as I worked with more and more organizations is, instead of having the technology slowing the flow, most organizations are still stuck in the product life cycle view where they don't move further down the deployment pipeline until they reach a phase in the software development life cycle, such as development complete. This is even true for organizations that consider themselves very mature in terms of adopting Agile. They batch up inventory and wait until they reach development complete and then they move large batches of inventory to the next stage of the deployment pipeline to start inspecting in quality. It's important to understand what's driving the timing. Is it technology, or is it a process like your product development life cycle? Once you have defined your deployment pipeline, starting with your architecture, measure how long it takes from a developer checking in code to getting into production to understand the cycle time.

Next, we need to look at how big a delay we have in feedback between when a developer writes the code and when they get the feedback that it has broken something. This is a big source of waste. As we're trying to improve the developers and build in quality, we want to give them that feedback as soon as possible. Once you have your deployment pipeline cycle time map, you know how long it takes to get to each environment. The next thing we want to know is what percentage of defects are being found in which environment. This tells us about the waste associated with feedback delay. You know how long it takes code to get to each environment, and you know what percentage of defects are found where. This measure provides a quantitative view of the waste associated with delay in feedback. Reducing this waste can be accomplished by finding defects further to the left in the deployment pipeline and/or by reducing the cycle time for code flowing through the different stages. In Figure 29 on page 118, where 60% of the defects are found four weeks after the developers have written the code, you can't expect them to get very good at building in quality.

Repetitive Task Defects

The triage of defects associated with repetitive task is another big source of waste that is easy to measure in organizations. If you have to triage the defects associated with the deployment, environment, or test, that should be considered waste. These are repetitive tasks that we can automate to make consistent and reliable. Every time we see a defect associated with repetitive tasks, we should look to fix it through automation once and for

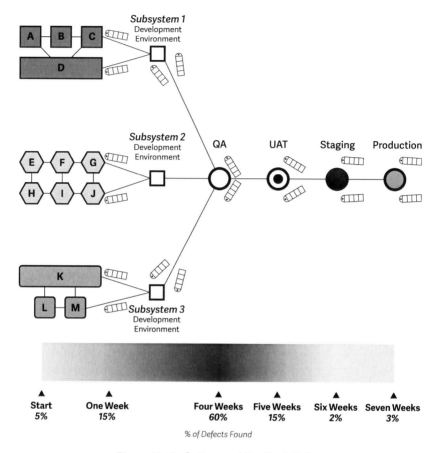

Figure 29: Cycle-time and Feedback Delay

all. We need to have appropriate defect tags so we can create Pareto charts like Figure 30 on page 119 that shows the source of errors with repetitive tasks for each environment in the deployment pipeline. This provides a clear metric of the waste that is reducing flow in the organization that we can use to drive improvements.

Product Control Charts

We also want to be measuring the waste associated with not building in quality. The product control charts show the regression test passing rates and the source of quality problems. We

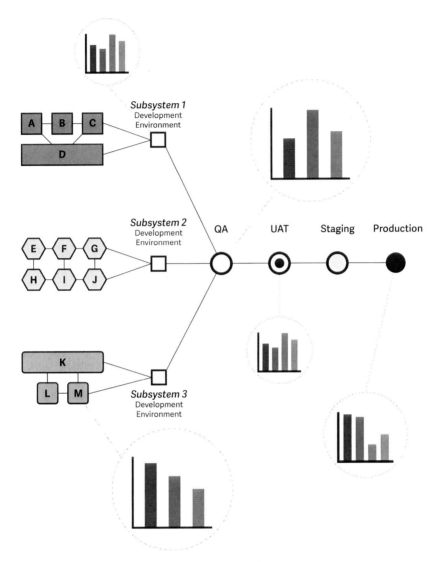

Figure 30: Defect Pareto Chart by Environment

want to look at the quality charts from the deployment pipeline at the right and work left. Our focus should be on identifying anything that we find further to the right that we could have found left on the deployment pipeline. This is another source of waste that we should be working to eliminate in the organization.

Branching

Software, once we've developed and qualified it, should, by its nature, be able to be used as many times as required. Those efficiencies start to fall apart anytime that we see branches in the code. Branches should be viewed as a big source of waste that should be minimized as much as possible. In the beginning, branches exist for a reason. We should work to understand that reason and work to address the issues so that the waste associated with duplication can be eliminated. The first step in achieving this is to making the branches visible like in Figure 31 below.

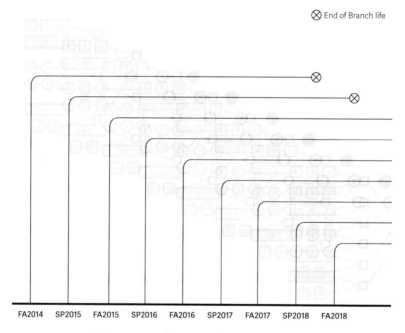

⊗ End of Branch life

| FA2014 | SP2015 | FA2015 | SP2016 | FA2016 | SP2017 | FA2017 | SP2018 | FA2018 |

Figure 31: Making Branching Waste Visible

Inventory Risk

The other challenge that we have in software development is that software habitually builds up inventory to process in large batches. This is traditionally the case where there are a lot of expensive manual tests. The natural tendency is to batch them together to keep test costs down because the costs associated with building, deploying, and testing one line of code change is the same as the cost to do the same with 100,000 lines of code change. Therefore, organizations often work to keep costs down by batching inventory together. This overlooks the inefficiencies that result from triaging these large batches. As we create new capabilities with an automated deployment pipeline and an automated, stable quality signal, we can start to change those economics and move to smaller batch sizes to improve the triage process.

Manufacturing taught us that the key to improving flow and quality is to keep work in process inventory as low as possible. This helps to reduce the risk of rework. It also improves the visibility of any issues that are impacting flow. The problem with software is that this inventory isn't very visible. Organizations batch up large amount of inventory on branches until they reach stages like development complete, then integrate it and inspect in quality. Manufacturing would never consider doing something like this. Every time they see inventory, they see risk they should be working to eliminate.

Inventory risk is the same with software, we just need to change the perception and make the inventory visible, which requires a metric. I don't like using lines of code turmoil to measure productivity because it encourages the problematic behavior of copying and pasting code. I do, however, believe that lines of code turmoil is a good measure of inventory in the system. Tracking it encourages everyone to check in new code and get it to trunk on a regular basis. Even if they don't, it at least encourages them not to copy and paste because that would just show more inventory that has not been integrated. To understand this inventory risk, we should be able look at our deployment pipeline and see how many lines of code changes are at each node of the deployment pipeline that have not been integrated into the overall system like in Figure 32 on page 122. We need to get used to thinking of that inventory not as an asset but as a risk like they do in manufacturing. The more inventory we have in the system, the more risk we have of waste slowing down flow.

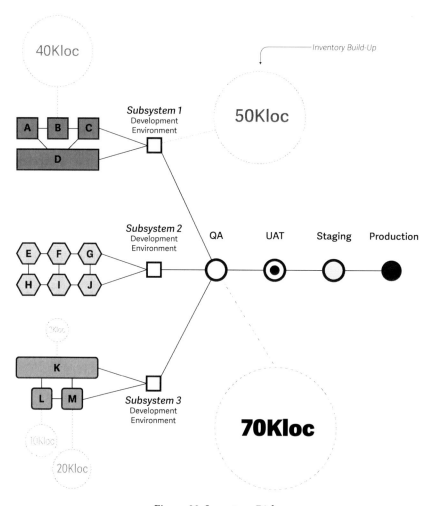

Figure 32: Inventory Risk

Shared Resources

A big source of waste in software development is handoffs where the work is waiting in queues. To reduce this waste, whenever possible, we should use whole product teams that can implement everything without handoffs. When we have to have shared resources, we need to ensure the development teams aren't slowed down waiting on these handoffs. In a large organization where we have shared resources, we need to make sure that we're measuring those teams based on their responsiveness instead of on inefficiencies, a principle Donald Reinertsen discusses in *The Principles of Product Development Flow* (Reinertsen 2009, chap. 7).

MTTR

When you do own deployment, the next metric that's important to capture and see is mean time to repair. If it's taking you a long time to repair and you're having a lot of issues in production, you're not going to be very efficient.

Summary

There is a lot that software can learn from manufacturing's systematic approach to continuous improvement. Most important is creating a culture where everyone is expected to contribute and is given the opportunity to do so. Software products and processes can and should be continually improved by providing a structured approach that enables everyone to participate.

The product can be improved, but very few organizations have developed the structure an A3 approach can provide. The architecture has significant impacts on the efficiencies of the deployment pipeline, but very few organizations think about it that way and are continually improving the design. The quality can be improved, but not that many organizations have a stable signal they are using to build in quality. Removing waste in the deployment pipeline can significantly improve flow and software productivity, but not very many organizations are focused here either. The opportunities for improvement are everywhere, but we need to shift the culture to focus on these opportunities and provide a systematic approach for improvements. These are the types of things we can and should be doing to continually improve the product and the process. The table on page 124 summarizes the metrics we can use to prioritize improvements and quantify the impact of changes.

	Metric	Intent
Product Metrics	Business Intent Metrics	Clarity of target and over delivery
	Featue usage	Measure over delivery
Process Metrics *Making the SW factory visible*	Deployment pipeline	Need to make our SW factories visible
	Branching	Waste assocaited with duplicate work
Build in Quality	Environment defect Pareto charts	Waste associated with errors in repetitive tasks
	Product Control charts	Progress in building in quality
	Feedback delay	Progress in helping developers improve
Flow	Cycle-time	Time to Value
	Inventory	Visibiity of Risk
	MTTR	Responsiveness

As this isn't enough alone, we also need to modify our approach to planning to take advantage of the flexibility software provides. In the next chapter, we will look more closely at planning and how to optimize it for software.

CHAPTER 8

Planning

The planning approaches used for software in most organizations are based on how it is done for other parts of the business. For example, in manufacturing product development you make long-range commitments to a specific deliverable on a specific date. Planning requires committing to doing something at a specific time. It's measured based on how well you meet the plan. Most organizations plan software that way. In software, however, once you have an automated deployment pipeline building in quality planning can move toward ensuring a prioritized backlog and releasing work at a rate that does not build up excess inventory.

As software capabilities improve in the ways we described in the previous chapters, the planning processes also needs to evolve to take advantage of these new capabilities. Similar to Goldratt's MRP example, as we change the capabilities, we also need to change the rules and our approach to planning because these areas have big opportunities for improvement. This is usually not one of the first places we think to start because most organizations have other, lower hanging fruit, but over time, as you start building in quality and improving the flow, getting additional improvements requires modifying the approaches to planning.

Manufacturing uses planning for product development and releasing work into production. The planning for product development is required for coordination. The planning for manufacturing is more about determining how to release work into production to optimize flow and ensuring excess inventory is not building up in the system.

Software has the same two needs, but people tend to just focus on the planning for product development because they are not thinking of software development as a manufacturing process. Where product development planning is required for coordination of physical products, in software we have deployment pipelines that can automate that coordination. This means we can take a very different approach to planning for product development. Product development planning is more about creating a prioritized backlog of work and optimizing flow.

For manufacturing of software, we need to think about how we release work into development to ensure we are not building up excess work in process. Software planning should address how to staff stable product teams that will take ownership for continually improving both the product and the process. Additionally, since one of the unique challenges with software is the over-delivery of features that are not used or don't meet the business's intent, the planning process needs to look across product teams and occasionally shift people to teams where they can have a more significant impact on the business.

Manufacturing Approach to Planning

Product development planning is really important for manufacturing products. In manufacturing, you're trying to coordinate bringing together a lot of different design pieces and manufacturing capabilities to ensure that you can assemble a working product. Manufacturing traditionally uses the phase gate R&D process for planning each phase to ensure that they're not committing to increased levels of investment risk before they know all the different pieces will work together. All the different parts of the organization are expected to commit to a plan and deliver on their commitments. The organization is measured on accuracy to plan because of the impact that one piece not being ready has on the rest of the system.

Toyota takes a little different approach with planning product development (Morgan and Liker 2006, chap. 5). Instead of planning all the details and showing exactly how they come together, the product owner plans integration points during development when they bring all the different pieces together to ensure everything is still working as intended. Everybody in the organization knows what needs to be delivered at those specific times, and missing those dates isn't acceptable. Therefore, the organization doesn't plan the details and coordination, but they do have high-level milestones that define integration points. If, at those specific intervals, everything comes together and is working, then they know they are on schedule. The teams are measured on the quality of their deliveries at the different integration stages instead of accuracy of plans.

Ensuring that everything is ready at either the different integration points or the stage gates is important for manufacturing product development because the commitment to investments goes up, and not having everything coordinated could mean that you start the manufacturing process before everything is ready. There are two approaches for large projects in manufacturing. The first is to plan all the details for every component in a Gantt chart and track all the schedules. The second approach is what Toyota does. These are two different approaches to planning. They are both focused on coordinating deliveries because that is important, but the Toyota approach is more modernized and has more frequent integrations.

Planning for manufacturing uses different approaches for releasing work into the system based on the application. Henry Ford used the linked assembly line with limited space. Goldratt used Drum Buffer Rope for releasing work into production. Taiichi Ohno used Kanban to further optimize the release of work between all the different processes. The key is to apply the systematic principle of limiting work in process by managing the release of work, but optimizing the approach to meet the needs of the specific application.

Unique Characteristics and Capabilities of Software Related to Planning

Software is unique in that you don't need planning to coordinate the integration of all the different pieces because a well-designed deployment pipeline for the entire system ensures that all the different pieces and parts are integrated, tested, and deployed on an ongoing basis. This means you don't need planning to provide that role. The deployment pipeline provides that function.

It is hard to measure the productivity of software, so most organizations focus on commitment to plan. To ensure they are delivering as much value as possible, this planning process turns into a bit of a negotiation between the business and the software teams. The software team does their best at planning. The business decides that is not enough and forces the software team to commit to more and then holds them accountable for delivering to that over-commitment. This conflict-driven approach to driving more throughput tends to create lots of waste, minimizing instead of maximizing value to the customer.

Software products can be released and then continually improved over time. For planning, we don't need to know exactly when all the different features will come together, we just need to be able to coordinate the date of the releases with marketing and work to a prioritize backlog.

The other thing that's unique with software development is the much higher degree of uncertainty in planning because the technology, process, and tools are changing so fast. Also, 50% of everything we develop is either never used or doesn't meet its business intent (Kohavi et al. 2009, sec. 5). As an industry, we tend to over-deliver features that are not used, and most teams have never seen a feature they didn't need.

Most IT organizations plan and staff based on capital projects. Teams are formed to deliver a given set of software for a given amount of time and money. These teams know they are going to be disbanded and don't have to provide support after the project is complete. Therefore, there is little, if any, focus on the continuous improvement of the process and product. This results in a lot of technical debt and products that are difficult to support.

Implications for Planning Software

Once you have an automated deployment pipeline with a product team that is focused on continuing to build in quality and improve flow, you can take a very different approach to planning to take advantage of this new capability. Instead of measuring teams based on accuracy to plan, you can shift to maximizing flow for a well-prioritized backlog. This enables the business and technology teams to work together to maximize value for the customer instead of working against each other in the traditional confrontational planning processes. The planning process then needs to change to focus on how work is released off the prioritized backlog to ensure excess inventory is not building up in the system. The planning process needs to include staffing stable product teams that will take ownership for continually improving both the product and the process. It also needs to look across these stable teams over time to see when it makes sense to shift people across teams to applications that can have a bigger impact on the business. These are really big changes that have to be adapted to the specific organization in question, so later in the section we will provide a case study for how it was approached by Mike Young at HP.

Maximizing Flow for a Prioritized Backlog

In manufacturing, we need accuracy of the plan to improve the efficiencies and effectiveness in the organization. The coordination of all the different physical pieces is important to avoid a lot of waste. In software, we use a stable automated deployment pipeline to coordinate the work for the various components and minimize waste. The software systems are integrated on a much more frequent basis. Therefore, to improve the efficiencies of the organization, it is much more important to maximize flow than to optimize for accuracy of plan.

Planning has traditionally also been used by businesses to ensure they are getting as much value as possible from software. They do this by negotiating with their partners to commit to as much as possible, then holding them accountable to that commitment. This approach is problematic because software planning is inherently inaccurate due to all the changes in technologies and processes we discussed earlier. It also isn't required because with software there are better ways to ensure the business is getting as much value as possible. Instead of focusing on commitment to plan, the business should be focused on holding the software teams accountable for maximizing flow. Then, business and software teams can work together on maximizing this flow instead of working against each other on a commitment to plan. Providing maximum customer value is the goal everyone is trying to achieve anyway, and focusing on flow does that while taking a lot of waste away from the negotiated planning process. Then from a planning perspective, the most important thing that we need to be doing is prioritizing the work that we're releasing into the development process and ensuring that we're releasing it in a way that doesn't build up excess inventory in the system.

Agile started changing the planning process to address these unique challenges and characteristics of software by working off of a prioritized backlog to ensure teams are delivering the most valuable features first and keeping the code base close to releasable so they can hit the release date with the features that are ready. Agile uses the burn down charts to avoid releasing too much work in the system and creating excess inventory.

Agile also focuses on delivering a minimal viable product for the first release so software teams can get feedback from customers to inform the next set of enhancements. From a planning perspective, the minimal viable product approach can also help coordinate with marketing on release dates as long as it is really minimal and the software organization can easily commit with less than 50% of its capacity. If it is not minimal and organizations are forced to commit over 50% of their capacity just to hit the minimal viable product on the given date, then the organizations tend to fall back on the destructive negative behavior of over-commitment and accountability to accuracy of plan. The planning process needs to ensure the business the product team will stay in place once the minimal viable product is delivered so they don't have to force everything into the first release. Additionally, both sides need to work together to maximize flow so the business sees how this new approach is meeting their goal of getting as much value as possible.

This change in approach for planning of software is probably one of the biggest fundamental shifts in mindsets that most traditional organizations need to make as they start competing more and more based on software. Everything else that they do in their organization is focused on committing to a plan and delivering to a plan because it is required for physical products. As these people start working and managing software projects in their organizations, they expect planning commitments to work the same way and deliver the same value as it does everywhere else.

They need to understand that software is different. The deployment pipeline is much more effective at coordinating the work across teams. The product can be continually improved with early and frequent releases. The planning process is much more uncertain, so instead of fighting that uncertainty, they should design their process to take advantage of the flexibility software provides. Instead of using planning as a negotiating tool to get teams to over-commit, business and software teams can work together to maximize flow of a prioritized backlog.

Releasing Work to Avoid Excess Work in Process (Inventory)

Manufacturing learned that maximizing flow requires managing the release of work into production to reduce the waste associated with excess inventory. Henry Ford limited inventory with a linked assembly line that had limited space. Taiichi Ohno used Kanban. Goldratt used Drum Buffer Rope. The key to each was limiting inventory in the system that was at risk of rework and making the issues that were impacting flow visible. For software, we can use the automated deployment pipeline to ensure all the inventory quickly flows from checked in to integrated and then tested in the broader system. We can also move the constraint to the development teams by removing waste in the deployment pipeline and then releasing work to the development teams at the rate they are completing work. This can be done using either Kanban or Drum Buffer Rope since they are essentially the same thing for the one step between ideation and development.

The amount of work invested in requirements is minimized until the teams are ready to start the work so we can take advantage of software's flexibility. The level of investment in requirements is a form of inventory for software. Manufacturing has learned to minimize inventory to reduce the waste associated with rework and expediting. In software, rework is reduced by not having big investments in requirements before developers are ready to engage and can ask the questions to get the requirements right the first time. Waste is reduced by not having to throw away big investments in requirements when the market changes and other requirements become more important. Waste can also be reduced when you don't feel compelled to deliver features that have big investments that aren't likely to deliver the intended results because of changes in the market. By keeping investments in requirements low until developers are ready to start working on them, the organization can take advantage of the flexibility software provides while minimizing the waste. It provides the business the flexibility to change priorities up until the developers start working on the requirements because there isn't the worry about throwing away significant amounts of work.

Product Teams

We want to be able to staff stable product teams so that they're taking ownership for continuously improving the product and the process. The traditional approach of staffing capital projects with teams that go away at the end of the project results in teams that leave lots of technical debt because they know they are not going to be around to continuously improve the product and use the process. Therefore, we want to make sure that we're able to staff product teams on an ongoing basis. We want these stable product teams to be able to pull work off a prioritized backlog and deliver independently as much as possible. If they need support from shared resources, we need to ensure those common resources do not slow them down. We want to make sure that those common resources have excess capacity. Don't manage those common resources based on efficiency, manage them based on responsiveness.

Capacity Adjustments

Software planning has a much higher degree of uncertainty than manufacturing. We can either try to reduce that uncertainty or develop a planning process that is designed to live with it. In manufacturing, we hold inventory at distribution centers because the demand variability is lower than at the store. With software, we can hold back committing long-range capacity to enable response to uncertainty. This capacity should be developers that have the experience to help across a broad range of applications. In this case, we staff the product teams with a stable set of developers over a long time horizon so they take ownership for continuous improvement of the product and process. We augment the stable product teams with more flexible resources for shorter periods of time. Just like with inventory, there will be a higher degree of uncertainty at the team level than there is at the organization level. If we fully commit all the resources at the team level for long time horizons, then we don't have the flexibility to respond to the unknown. Instead, we need to hold back some excess capacity in terms of funding or developers to help out the teams that ran into unforeseen challenges or came up with potentially great new ideas so we have the flexibility to respond to software's uncertainty. This is accomplished by not committing all of our capacity to long-range plans.

We need a planning process that is able to look across the different development teams to understand what they've been able to deliver and the current challenges, and to compare their plans to the business value. Then, we are able to move the flexible resources across development to teams to where they are most needed. This helps to address the over-delivery of features where we end up with more than 50% of capabilities that are never used or don't meet the business intent (Kohavi et al., 2009). From a planning process perspective, we want to be looking at what we're spending with each different product team on a quarterly basis to see how well we're doing with moving the product metrics that we define for continuous improvement. We need to review the backlog to understand the value of future investment, then we can move the flexible resources to the opportunity that has the biggest potential for improving the business as necessary.

This focus on taking advantage of the unique characteristics of software and fundamentally changing how we do commitments and planning for software is not usually one of the first challenges organizations address. They tend to focus on taking waste out of the deployment pipeline and building in quality. When that is working well, it is easier to see that one of the next big opportunities is improving how they prioritize and release work into the system.

HP CASE STUDY OF OPTIMIZING PLANNING FOR SOFTWARE

HP is a good example of how to optimize planning for the unique characteristics and capabilities of software. The first two to three years of the transformation, we didn't need to invest in changes to the planning process (Gruver, Young, and Fulghum 2013, chap. 7). We were working to ensure that all the old features were available on the new architecture, so our whole focus was on throughput. As we got our first release out the door and after the deployment pipeline was mature, we started looking at new feature requests, and the planning process became more important. Mike Young took the approach of fundamentally changing how we did planning. When we were using 150% of our capacity just to ship products and we needed to make a commitment to build a new manufacturing line 18 months in the future, we really couldn't change our planning process. As we improved our efficiencies with the re-architecture and automated our deployment pipeline, releasing new products with existing functionality required less than 50% of our capacity. This enabled us to fundamentally change our planning process. We limited the amount of our capacity that we would commit over different time horizons as shown in Figure 33.

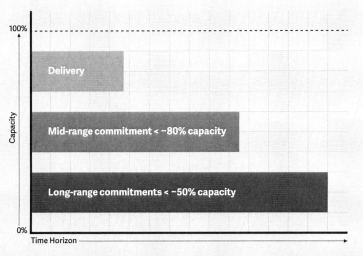

Figure 33: Incrementally Commiting Capacity Over Time

For the long-range commitments, we would look at all the new capabilities unique to that product and ensure there weren't any big surprises that would spike basic product support to over 50% of our capacity. This was a pretty straightforward analysis that let us know we could support the long-range commitment to manufacturing. We still didn't know the other features that would ship with the product, but that wasn't really required that far in the future.

Next, we focused on the mid-range commitments for the next six months. The product marking organization prioritized the high-level initiatives that they wanted to message for the next product release window. Then, the system engineers would breakdown the initiatives into a high-level estimate of how many resources it would require from each team as shown in Figure 34 on page 137.

With this easy-to-create chart, we were able to say to the marketing organization, "You can count on initiatives A through G happening because we have plenty of capacity. Initiatives K through M probably are not going to happen, so you should start the grieving process. Initiatives H through J may or may not happen depending on our throughput." Additionally, the initiatives closer to H were more likely to happen, so marketing needed to focus on the relative priorities in this group between H and J because that was where it would matter. Spending time arguing if C or D was a higher priority wasn't a good use of marketing time because they were both going to happen. This chart also enabled engineering leadership to look at the demand across teams to see if we needed to shift resources. For a very small investment in planning, we were able to give the marketing organization a reasonable idea of what to expect.

The planning for the initiatives would stay in this state until the developers were freed up and ready for new work, then we would hold the feature kick-off meeting that included the marketing representative, the system engineer that pro-

Spr11 1–N High-Level Risk/Resource Analysis

Rank	Initiative	Component 1 (25–30)	Component 2 (20–25)	Component 3 (30–40)	Component 4 (30–40)	Component 5 (20–30)	Component 6 (20–30)	Component 7 (20–30)	Component 8 (15–25)	Component 10 (15–25)	Component 11 (20–30)	Component 12 (20–30)	Other Teams	Total
				High-Level Estimate—FW Engineering Months										
1	Initiative A			21			5	3		1				30
2	Initiative B	3							4				17	24
3	Initiative C		5							2	1	1		9
4	Initiative D							10		2	2	2		16
5	Initiative E					20						3	5	28
6	Initiative F	23							5	6		2		36
7	Initiative G									2				2
8	Initiative H											5		5
9	Initiative I												3	3
10	Initiative J		20	27			17			39	17	21	9	133
11	Initiative K			3	30		3		3	14			23	71
12	Initiative L									2				2
13	Initiative M	3						10		6	6	6		31
		29	25	51	30	20	25	23	12	74	26	38	59	401

↑
Light Weight Estimate for Initiatives

Figure 34: Light Weight Planning for Mid-Range Commitments

vided the estimates, and the product development teams that owned the delivery. The marketing representative would review what was expected with the initiative and answer any questions from the developers. The system engineers would review how they felt the design would work with the estimates and answer any questions. The developers then would break down the initiative into story points they would deliver.

Then, as you can see in Figure 35, we would track story points delivered over time, not as a measure of productivity but simply to give us a rough feel for how much was getting through the organization. We tried to keep the story points at roughly an engineer effort for a week, but there was a fair amount of variability. We did have to intervene with one team because they were breaking story points into about a half a day of work for an engineer, and it was skewing our high-level view, but for the most part, we let teams work at a detail that made sense to them. As we tracked this story throughput, we could get a quick view of what was likely to happen. The highest priority stories that were low on the bar chart could be counted on to happen. The stories that were very high on the bar chart were probably not going to happen. The stories in the middle might happen depending on throughput.

These approaches freed up a lot of extra capacity. We went from using 20% of our capacity for planning down to 5%. This freed up an extra 15% of the capacity of the organization that could be used to focus on delivering value to our customers. The early stages of planning took a lot less effort because we were not committing all of our capacity. In fact, the final 20% of the capacity with feature stories we didn't commit to a plan. We just focused on throughput of the prioritized stack and the graph in Figure 35 on page 139 as a predictor of when things might get delivered. The marketing organization and development were both focused on doing whatever possible to increase the throughput because everyone could see their stories getting closer to the done line. It wasn't development and marketing working against each other to force commitment to an unrealistic plan. It was development and marketing working together on a prioritized stack and working to improve throughput. It also provided marketing with a lot more flexibility to respond to changes in the market. As long as the development teams hadn't started the work of breaking the initiatives into stories, marketing was free to change priorities because we had so little invested. It meant that we didn't have the detailed plans that we did before and the belief in the accuracy that had provided. But the reality was that the accuracy hadn't been much higher than what we were providing with the new process, even with a much smaller investment.

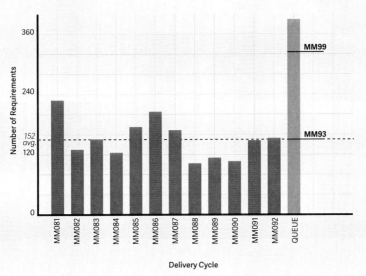

Figure 35: Tracking Delivery versus Planning for the Rest of the Capacity

This was a big fundamental change for an organization that had been doing physical product development for years. It took a little while for people to get used to it, but once they saw the advantages, they accepted it and saw the benefits that it could provide. These are the types of things that you need to do differently with software development to take advantage of its unique characteristics and capabilities.

Summary

Changing the approach for software planning is probably one of the hardest cultural shifts for large organizations. As a result, it is probably not one of the first challenges organizations will address. It is usually addressed after organizations stabilize the deployment pipeline and build in quality. At this point, it is probably one of the next biggest opportunities. Improvements in planning can provide significant benefits.

Changing how organizations plan requires a very different approach. Instead of focusing on coordination of the different components, software can rely on the deployment pipeline for coordination on a much more frequent basis. Instead of commitment and accuracy to plan between software and the business, they can work together on maximizing the flow of value. This requires a prioritized backlog and focus on continuous improvement of the product and the process. These are significant changes for most organizations but can make organizations much more efficient and take advantage of software's flexibility.

CHAPTER 9

Systematic Approaches for Software Improvement

Manufacturing has very systematic approaches that have driven dramatic improvements over time. These are based on common principles with the practices then being fine-tuned to fit the application. Training and certification requires not just understanding the concepts but proving you can apply the principles to deliver improvements for the business. If software is going to achieve the dramatic improvements that manufacturing has, it is going to need a similar systematic approach based on principles. These principles can't just be copied from manufacturing—they need to be tuned to address the unique capabilities and characteristics of software. The goal of this chapter is to lay the foundation for that systematic approach. It is not intended to be a static answer or THE approach. The purpose is to lay the foundation that can be used, improved, and fine-tuned by lots of great minds in different organizations similar to what happened in manufacturing over decades. Manufacturing learned over time that the approaches for applying the principles really depend on the application. The same will be true for software, so here we will start with manufacturing examples of how the principles were tuned for different applications.

Creating a systematic approach for improvements is going to be a big cultural change that is best led from the top. Therefore, we will review the executive's role. They need to decide it is important enough to lead. They need to segment their different applications into different deployment pipelines because different applications will require the approaches to be modified to meet their unique challenges. It can't be a maturity model or just replicating the approaches of other successful teams. They need to prioritize the deployment pipelines they want to improve. And they need to assign leaders that are responsible for systematically improving those pipelines.

The leaders for each prioritized pipeline need to lead the systematic improvement of both the product and process for their deployment pipeline. The principles for the product's continuous improvement need to be based on the A3 charts and the scientific method. The process improvements need to be based on the principles of optimizing flow using the Theory of Constraints. They need work with their teams to teach these principles and create a prioritized backlog of improvements they believe will provide the biggest benefits.

The planning process needs to involve staffing stable product teams to ensure there is a focused group engaged in driving continuous improvement for each deployment pipeline they want to improve. The executive team needs to be looking across the different deployment pipelines to ensure people are moved over time to applications where they can have the biggest impact on the business. Everyone needs to have a role and a way to contribute if organizations are going to embrace these new ways of working. If training is provided it needs to go beyond ensuring people understand the concepts to ensuring people can use the principles to deliver measurable improvements.

Systematic Approach for Manufacturing

The approach used for improving systems has a big impact on the results. Manufacturing's focus on cost accounting and efficiencies drove suboptimal results compared to optimizing flow through the Theory of Constraints or Lean Six Sigma.

The implementation you choose for applying the principles really depends on the system you are trying to optimize. Donald Reinertsen points out that the TOC approach of Drum Buffer Rope is suboptimal to the Kanban approach because just releasing work into production based on the bottleneck does not take into account how inventory flows through the entire process and can result in simply moving bottlenecks around (Reinertsen 2009, chap. 6). In a stable, high-volume manufacturing process, you can gain additional benefits by coordinating the flow of work between all the different workstations with Kanban.

At the same time, Goldratt does a very good job of pointing out that Kanban is designed to work in an environment where the products and process do not change frequently and where there is stability in overall demand (Goldratt 2006). In the case of Hatachi, with short product life cycles and lots of demand variability, the Kanban approach of buffering inventory between every step would result in too much inventory and scrap at product end of life. For that situation, the Drum Buffer Rope approach is much more appropriate.

The most appropriate approach for improvement depends on the application. Therefore, it is important to focus on the principles and not the specific approach. Instead of sub-optimizing different parts of the system, we need to focus on flow through the entire system. Ford optimized flow based on space. Ohno used Kanban, and Goldratt used Drum Buffer Rope. All approaches were focused on similar principles but optimized the implementation for the specific application.

Developing a systematic approach for driving improvements in software needs to focus on the higher-level principles that allow optimization of the implementation for specific applications. It has to be more than simply following the Agile rituals to achieve great results. The Agile principles are great, but too many implementations get lost in the rituals. It has to be more than just a collection of all the great ideas that have been implemented by different groups and captured by the DevOps community.

It needs to be more than just benchmarking what all the best companies are doing and starting with the most common best in class practices that you haven't yet implemented. These are all great improvements in the right direction, but if we are going to engineer a more systematic approach to improving software, we need to start with high-level principles that can be optimized for specific applications.

There is a lot we can learn from Deming about building in quality versus the current approach of delayed inspection and rework, but it is a limited view of the system. There is also a lot we can learn from Ohno about a systematic approach to the scientific method and engaging the entire organization in continuous improvement, but the scientific method doesn't work as well for software process improvement because it is hard to measure flow. In addition, there is a lot we can learn from Goldratt about understanding the constraint in the system to improve flow, but this is different from how we think about it in manufacturing because with digital assets you can build, deploy, and test 1 line of code and 100,000 lines of code in the same amount of time and for the same cost.

Systematic Approach for Software

The first step is creating a culture of continuous improvement that needs to start at the top and should include the expectation of a structured approach. The structured approach needs to start with the principles that can be modified to fit the specific applications. The systematic approach for improving software development requires improving both the product and the process. These two things differ significantly enough that they require different principles to drive improvements. For continuous improvement of the product, the principles can leverage the Kata process and the scientific method. This doesn't work as well for process improvement because the product and process are changing at the same time and the flow is hard to measure. Therefore, the principle that is more appropriate for software development process is to focus on improving flow using the Theory of Constraints.

Culture of Continuous Improvement

Creating a culture of continuous improvement needs to start at the top and flow down through the organization similar to the Kata process. The executives have a key role in creating the culture, focusing the organization on where to start, and staffing the leadership of the continuous improvement efforts for each deployment pipeline. The leadership of each deployment pipeline needs to work with the organization to use a systematic approach to improving both the product and the process.

Executive's Role

An ongoing focus on continuous improvement of both the product and the process using a systematic approach is the biggest thing missing in software development. If this is going to change for most organizations, it needs to be led by the executives, like Taiichi Ohno did at Toyota. He made it clear that it was everybody's job to not only do his or her job, but also to continue to improve how the job was done (Rother 2010). He also provided a structured approach for how everybody should be doing continuous improvement. If software organizations are going to change, they will benefit significantly from that type of executive leadership willing to help drive the change and champion it into the organization. The executives need to make it clear that continuous improvement is an expectation, but they also need to provide the bandwidth and structure for doing it.

For small, loosely coupled teams that can work independently, executives should set the expectation and then work to understand the barriers that exist across the organization and help to remove them. For larger, tightly coupled systems, this is a more complex process. The types of things that you do to improve these tightly coupled systems are really going to depend on the specific application and the waste that is slowing down their flow. Allowing these teams to fine-tune the improvements they prioritize based on the need of the business provides a couple of advantages. First, it's going to ensure that the improvements are not based on some generic business maturity model, but on the impact that it can have on the effectiveness of the organization. Second, if we let the teams drive their improvement based on what they see can have the most value, we're going to get them to take more ownership and have more passion about ensuring that their ideas are successful. It's what Taiichi Ohno did with the Kata process. Instead of doing what Fredrick Winslow Taylor did in terms of telling everybody what to do, Ohno created a process that engaged everyone. We're going to be more successful in getting that personal ownership and implementations that fit the applications if we can go to smaller deployment pipelines as much as possible.

The executives need to look across their organization and identify the different deployment pipelines that exist and then segment these as small as possible. However, if the architecture of the applications are tightly coupled to a point where they need to be developed, qualified, and deployed as one system, then that's one deployment pipeline. After separating applications in the organization into as many different deployment pipelines as possible, executives should prioritize the different deployment pipelines that can add the most value to the business for starting down the continuous improvement journey.

They also need to assign the leadership teams to improve these applications and processes. This could be an individual that has overall leadership across the deployment pipeline. It may be individuals that work in different areas of the organization, such as development, quality assurance, security, and operations, that have to work together to improve the deployment pipeline. They all need to come together to drive a common set of priorities into the organizations if it is going to see the types of improvement required. The executive should expect these teams to be holding monthly checkpoints where they review what got done, what didn't get done, what they learned, and what they're going to do next. Executives should attend these checkpoints to see the progress the teams are making. They should also be looking for opportunities to remove any bottlenecks or barriers that are getting in the way of the organizations making progress.

The Deployment Pipeline Leadership Team's Role

The leadership team assigned to each deployment pipeline should create a formal process for continuous improvement. As discussed in *Leading the Transformation*, this should include clear objectives and monthly checkpoints to review progress (Gruver and Mouser 2015, chap. 4). They need to work to ensure there is a prioritized backlog of improvements that will make the biggest difference from both a product improvement and a process improvement perspective. They need to ensure that they're teaching their teams the proper structured approaches to continuous improvement. This training needs to go beyond making sure they understand the concepts to ensuring they can successfully apply the concepts to deliver measurable improvements. Similar to what manufacturing did with 6 Sigma Green Belt and Black Belt training. They need to be reviewing progress that the teams are making on an ongoing basis and continually removing roadblocks that are getting in the way of the organization making progress.

SYSTEMATIC APPROACH FOR PRODUCT CONTINUOUS IMPROVEMENT

The leadership team for the specific deployment pipeline needs to create the A3 charts for continues improvement of the product. They need to align with organizations on the metrics that they're trying to achieve and the ability to capture those metrics. They need to capture the metrics that show feature usage so that they know how much of what they're creating is actually being used because that's one of the biggest sources of waste in software development. They need to be able to track the impact on the business intent metrics from release to release. They're constantly working with their teams and partners to ensure that there is a well-groomed prioritized backlog for work that will improve the product the most.

SYSTEMATIC APPROACH FOR PROCESS CONTINUOUS IMPROVEMENT

This leadership team also needs to make sure that the team is aligned on continually improving the process. The first step here is ensuring that the digital factory is visible. Start by documenting the current architecture and deployment pipeline. Look at all the metrics discussed earlier in terms of the cycle time from code check-ins to being in production. Look at the delay in feedbacks. Where are defects found, and how long is that after the individuals have been writing code? Look at the Pareto charts of the repetitive task defects. These are the types of things that can be automated out of the system. They're a source of waste because people have to triage and fix things that we can automate and fix once and for all. Create the product control charts to understand the quality issues. Document where branches create duplicate work in our deployment pipelines and why. Map the inventory of lines of code turmoil not integrated on top of the deployment pipeline to highlight that risk. Look for delays faced by the development teams as a result of handoffs, and be sure to measure common resources based on responsiveness. For organizations that own deployment and operations, look at mean time to repair. These are the types of metrics to help highlight the biggest sources of waste in the organization that are slowing down flow.

Next, one of the biggest breakthroughs in software development that enables improving flow in the deployment pipeline is the ability to build in quality. The first step for most organizations is working through the process to ensure there is a stable quality signal. The types of things that different deployment pipelines find that are causing instability are going to vary. Those specific sources of instability need to drive the improvement priorities. It is not just a simple matter of following a maturity model and implementing what worked for others. It is going to require the hard work of root cause analysis and fixing issues specific to the application.

The next bottleneck that occurs for most organizations is the amount of time and effort it takes to triage and fix defects. Because this is the biggest constraint, the next biggest opportunity is to start building in quality. Create quality gates and move to smaller batch sizes that are easier to triage. Ensuring the signal is stable and working to build in quality are the first two steps that commonly have the biggest impact on improving the flow through organizations with large, tightly coupled systems.

After those first two steps, the next improvements are very dependent on the application. Use the Theory of Constraints to look at the next most important things to fix. Look at the metrics for measuring waste and making it visible. Prioritize the improvements based on these metrics. When making changes designed to eliminate waste, measure the impact and make it visible in the organization. We should use the Theory of Constraints to prioritize the things that are slowing down the flow of the organization and eliminate waste. Just like with manufacturing, the approaches are going to depend on the specific applications and the sources of waste.

The types of things that show up when doing this analysis are going to be very different depending on the architecture and type of application. For a loosely coupled system, the architecture is unlikely to be the source of constraint. Rather, it is typically handoffs across teams or different constraints outside the team that they can't control that need to be removed.

For tightly coupled systems, the constraint tends to be the lack of quality and batching up inventory. The focus in this case is on reducing inventory and moving to smaller batch sizes that are more efficient to triage. As we start building in quality, there are also opportunities to look at decoupling the system so smaller teams that are loosely coupled can work independently. This can either be through micro-services getting spun off or breaking the large monolith to smaller subsystems that have smaller teams that can move independently.

There are additional challenges if you're creating applications that customers deploy and customize in their datacenters. From the developers' perspective, it is the number of branches that end up having to be supported in these applications. On the customer's side, it is the difficulties of upgrading and adding customizations. We should prioritize improving the architecture to enable decoupling between the application and customizations, enabling the customizations to be automatically applied and stored in the SCM, and providing the framework for automated testing. For these types of applications, those are frequently the biggest barriers to flow.

Embedded applications have different challenges. The goal is to enable as much of the code as possible to be developed on the efficiencies that come with simulators. We must create a very clear hardware abstraction layer and move as much code above that line as possible. It is also important to find as many defects as far left on the deployment pipeline as possible because that's where the testing, triage, and defect fixing isn't duplicated across a bunch of different environments. This requires improvements in simulators and emulators.

If you don't own deployment, there are different challenges. If getting customers to update to the latest code is the biggest bottleneck, you can assume that their update frequency is something you can't change like most of the automobile industry or work to change it to provide a competitive advantage like Tesla.

Ideally, we're trying to take all the waste and inefficiencies out of the deployment pipeline and move them to the development teams. Once we've done that, we can focus on doing everything we possibly can to make sure those development teams are being more productive.

The deployment pipeline leadership team needs to be looking at the backlog associated with continuous improvement of the product and process. They need to be making sure that there's a very accurate view of the top priorities that the organization feels will have the biggest impact for that specific deployment pipeline.

Planning

The leadership team and the leaders of the deployment pipelines have different roles in planning. The role of the leadership team over the deployment pipeline is to drive the continuous improvement of their product and process. To ensure they have momentum in this continuous improvement journey, they must make sure that they are advertising the gains of the improvements. They need to ensure they have a very good, prioritized backlog that the team should be working on to drive the improvement.

The executive leadership team needs to be able to look across the different deployment pipelines in the organization to allocate resources and prioritize work across the system. They need to be doing this because one of the biggest challenges that we have with software is we tend to over-deliver features to point of diminishing returns. Any good leadership team of a deployment pipeline should always have a backlog that they believe will make the biggest difference. The role of the leadership team is to be looking across those different deployment pipelines and seeing if the money would be better spent somewhere else. We still need to staff stable product teams at some level. But as the leadership team looks across the deployment pipelines and their ability to drive their business intent metrics, they may decide that there are better opportunities for different applications. Their role is to be constantly looking across the system and trying to find those opportunities and shift resources to take advantage of the flexibility software can provide.

Summary

Manufacturing has done a great job of driving a culture of continuous improvement and creating a systematic way of improving based on principles. Software development teams can learn a lot from manufacturing's approach. It needs to start with the executives developing a culture and expectation of continuous improvement and staffing teams with people who are going to lead these changes. These organizations need a systematic approach for prioritizing improvements to achieve product and process continuous improvement. Product continuous improvement can benefit from the rigor an A3 type process provides, while process continuous improvement should be focused on flow, using a Theory of Constraints approach. The leaders of the deployment pipeline need to be constantly grooming their backlog for the most valuable ideas. The executives need to be looking across different teams and seeing if different deployment pipelines are starting to over-deliver features and reach a point of diminishing returns. This systematic approach of continuous improvement for software development can and should have the same impact that it's had on manufacturing organizations.

CHAPTER 10

Summary

The goal of this book has been to provide a framework for a more systematic approach for managing software, an approach that organizations can use to prioritize and track the impact of improvements. Certainly we can't provide all the answers for how to engineer the digital transformation, but hopefully it helps people understand that there can and should be a different approach to engineering software than currently exists. We need to challenge and inspire the creative minds in software and the best minds in process engineering to work together so that over time they can develop and optimize approaches specifically for the unique characteristics and capabilities of software that will deliver the necessary and long-awaited breakthroughs in software development.

The manufacturing industry has a long history of continuous improvement that can and should be leveraged for software. However, we need to realize that digital assets are different, so the exact same approach won't work. Software has been modifying its approaches to address its unique capabilities and characteristics. There have been modifications from Agile, Lean software development, DevOps, and others. These initiatives are fundamentally changing software development to address its unique characteristics and capabilities.

Software doesn't yet have a very systematic approach to improvements. It is mostly about adopting the latest practices and certifying that people understand the concepts. As an industry, we've made some progress, but what would the manufacturing leaders think if they looked closely at how most software organizations are working today?

Would Deming be proud if he realized that we're manually doing repetitive tasks instead of automating them with DevOps? How would he feel about the fact that we're inspecting in quality and staging up huge batches of inventory to inspect in quality all at once at specific milestones? It is so problematic that we design hardening phases into our schedules instead of building in quality from the beginning. I am not sure if Deming would be very impressed with software's approach to quality.

How would Taiichi Ohno feel if he realized that in software development, we don't have a structured approach to continuous improvement that involves everybody? Even worse than that, what would he think if he knew that when team members find things that they know need fixing, we don't even give them the time to make improvements? We design our projects with end dates instead of taking advantage of the continuous improvement opportunities that exist with the product itself. I'm not sure Taiichi Ohno would feel that we have done a very good job of applying his Kata to software.

Do we think Goldratt would be proud of the fact that we haven't understood the breakthroughs that moving from physical to digital provides? That we've left the bottleneck with repetitive manual tasks that could be automated? Once we create the deployment pipeline and are able to build in quality, we aren't changing the rules to require running the automated testing on a more frequent basis to address the triage bottleneck. After all his work on flow versus cost accounting, how do you think he would feel about software development measuring teams on their accuracy to plan instead of on flow of value just because the flow is hard to measure?

We've made some fundamental changes with software, but when we look at it through these thinkers' eyes, I don't think they'd be very proud of what we've accomplished. For software development, we need a much more systematic approach to product and process improvement. It needs to be more than just implementing the latest rituals and hoping they provide some benefits for the business. It needs to start with a culture of continuous improvement that includes everybody. We need more than just the best ideas. We need to get people committed to embracing these new ways of working and championing the ideas that they have for improvement. We need to get much more structured in using the scientific approach for product continuous improvement. For process continuous improvement, we need to be focused on flow and building in quality. The fact that flow with software is hard to measure is no excuse. We can still measure the waste that is slowing flow and use that to prioritize improvements and quantify the impact of the changes.

In some respects, it feels like we face a monumental task and a long way to go for software organizations, but we should be hopeful. There are large organizations that have proven to be very successful. Google, Amazon, and others are showing that it's possible to come up with very efficient and effective approaches to developing software.

However, while it is possible, it is a significant challenge for the majority of large traditional software organizations. They're going to need a systematic approach if they're going to improve at the rate that's required to stay in business and competitive. They're going to need inspired leaders to help lead the change and teach the organization how to apply these systematic approaches to continually improving. The challenge for software is to find those people who are willing to lead the digital transformation and develop the engineering rigor to continue to improve the systematic approaches to improving how we manage digital assets in the knowledge-based economy.

Hopefully this book has laid the foundation for creating a systematic approach to improving software development that can be leveraged and improved. The approaches broadly used in manufacturing took generations and numerous thought leaders to fine-tune and improve. Software will need similar efforts to create approaches as valuable as what has been accomplished in manufacturing. We can learn from manufacturing's efforts and leverage as many as possible, but we also need to understand that software is a different beast that will require different approaches. My hope is that this book has helped lay the foundation to start that journey.

I hope you found the ideas in *Engineering the Digital Transformation* helpful and that you will put the systematic approaches to good use.

I love to hear from readers, so please email me with success stories and questions at gary@garygruver.com.

If you can think of others who would benefit from this content, please share an excerpt with them by visiting **http://bit.ly/ GruverExcerpt**. Enter price as $0 and then enter an email address to receive the file for immediate download.

In addition, the excerpt includes a 10% discount code for the purchase of the full-length ebook on Gumroad. I hope you find this useful, and thank you for helping spread the word.

—Gary Gruver

References

Ambler, Scott W. and Pramod J. Sadalage. 2006. *Refactoring Databases: Evolutionary Database Design*. Upper Saddle River, NJ: Addison-Wesley.

Beyer, Betsy et al., ed. 2016. *Site Reliability Engineering*. Sebastopol, CA: O'Reilly Media, Inc.

Davis, Cornelia. 2018. "Taking Ops & Infrastructure from Iterative to Functional, Just Like Dev." YouTube video. Posted by IT Revolution October 27, 2018. https://www.youtube.com/watch?v=R1RDhUf1Go4&feature=youtu.be.

Deming, W. Edwards. 1982. *Out of the Crisis*. Cambridge, MA: Massachusetts Institute of Technology, Center for Advanced Educational Services.

Edwards, Damon. 2012. "The (Short) History of DevOps." YouTube video. Posted by Damon Edwards September 17, 2012. https://www.youtube.com/watch?v=o7-IuYS0iSE&feature=youtu.be

Goldratt, Eliyahu M., and Jeff Cox. 2004. *The Goal: A Process of Ongoing Improvement*. Third Revision. Great Barrington, MA: The North River Press Publishing Corporation.

Goldratt, Eliyahu M. 2005. *Beyond the Goal: Theory of Constraints.* Read by the author. United States: Gildan Audio.

Goldratt, Eliyahu M. 2006. "Standing on the Shoulders of Giants: Production Concepts versus Production Applications, The Hitachi Tool Engineering Example." Goldratt Consulting. https://www.goldrattconsulting.com/webfiles/fck/files/Standing-on-the-Shoulders-of-Giants.pdf.

Gruver, Gary, Mike Young, and Pat Fulghum. 2013. *A Practical Approach to Large-Scale Agile Development: How HP Transformed LaserJet FutureSmart Firmware.* New Jersey: Addison Wesley.

Gruver, Gary, and Tommy Mouser. 2015. *Leading the Transformation: Applying Agile and DevOps Principles at Scale.* Portland, OR: IT Revolution.

Gruver, Gary. 2016. *Starting and Scaling DevOps in the Enterprise.* United States: BookBaby.

Highsmith, Jim. 2001. "History: The Agile Manifesto." Agilemanifesto.org. http://agilemanifesto.org/history.html.

Hognose. 2014. "Eli Whitney and Interchangeable Parts." *WeaponsMan.* May 29, 2014. http://weaponsman.com/?p=14382.

Humble, Jez, Joanne Molesky, and Barry O'Reilly. 2015. *Lean Enterprise: How High Performance Organizations Innovate at Scale.* Sebastopol, CA: O'Reilly Media, Inc.

Kohavi, Ronny et al. 2009. "Online Experimentation at Microsoft." Ai.stanford.edu. Accessed April 17, 2019. https://ai.stanford.edu/~ronnyk/ExPThinkWeek2009Public.pdf.

Lévénez, Éric. 2018. "Computer Languages History." Levenez.com. Last updated August 12, 2018. https://www.levenez.com/lang/.

Morgan, James M., and Jeffrey K. Liker. 2006. *The Toyota Product Development System: Integrating People, Process and Technology.* New York, New York: Productivity Press.

Morgan, Jeff. 2017. Cucumber & Cheese. Leanpub.

Narayan, Sriram. 2018. "Products Over Projects." MartinFowler. com. February 20, 2018. https://martinfowler.com/articles /products-over-projects.html.

Poppendieck, Mary, and Tom Poppendieck. 2003. *Lean Software Development: An Agile Toolkit.* United States: Addison-Wesley.

Prugh, Scott, and Brian Clark. 2018. "CSG: Product Management Meets DevOps." YouTube video. Posted by IT Revolution October 24, 2018. https://youtu.be/tgf_D2DUlJ0.

Reinertsen, Donald G. 2009. *The Principles of Product Development Flow: Second Generation Lean Product Development.* Redondo Beach, CA: Celeritas Publishing.

Rother, Mike. 2010. *Toyota Kata: Managing People for Improvement, Adaptiveness and Superior Results.* United States: Rother & Company, LLC.

Sobek, Durward K., and Art Smalley. 2008. *Understanding A3 Thinking: A critical Component of Toyota's PDCA Management System.* New York, NY; Productivity Press.

Wikipedia. 2019. "Cost Accounting." Wikipedia. last modified March 23, 2019. https://en.wikipedia.org/wiki /Cost_accounting.

———. 2019. "Frederick Winslow Taylor." Wikipedia. last modified March 20, 2019. https://en.wikipedia.org/wiki /Frederick_Winslow_Taylor.

Youel, Ted, Gary Gruver, and Jeff Keyes. 2018. "Leading the Transformation: Stories from the Trenches." YouTube video. Posted by Plutora November 29, 2018. https://www.youtube. com/watch?v=j5coOKImM6U.

Acknowledgments

Many people have contributed to this book. I would like to thank everyone I have worked with over the years that have helped me better understand how to develop software. The ideas shared in this book are accumulations of everything I have learned working with each of you to better understand how we improve our approaches to developing software. Without these discussions, debates, and experiments my understanding and the content of this book would not be as complete.

I would especially like to thank Jim Highsmith for a wonderful foreword. He has helped me from the beginning of my publishing career. Without his help I don't think I would have ever gotten started. He helped me figure out how to get published and introduced me to the Agile community. I can't thank him enough for everything he has done.

I would like to thank Ted Youel for sharing the story of his journey as a case study so people can better understand what a transformation looks like inside a large organization and the benefits it can provide.

I would also like to thank everyone that has taken the time to provide feedback on early versions of the book (in alphabetical order): Tom Beckwith, Kent Eckert, Bryan Finster, Martin Fowler, Jim Highsmith, Basheer Janjua, John Jeremia, Greg Lonnon,

Tommy Mouser, Rob Parkhill, Mark Segal, Mike Young, Ted Youel. Your input significantly improved the final product.

I would also like to thank the publishing team that helped make this book possible. Starting with Kate Sage the editor. She helped lead me through the process of creating a book once again. She forced me to provide clarity of thought and crispness of message. I can't ever imagine trying to write another book without her help. I would like to thank Devon Smith for his work on the graphics. I am not a visual person but I understand it is important. It is nice to have a person on the team that can cover for my visual weaknesses. And finally I would like to thank my marketing team of Robyn Crummer-Olson and Kristen Ludwigsen. A book is only valuable if people read it. They have done an outstanding job of helping me understand how to best reach the people that can benefit most from this content.

And, thanks to Bob Seastrom for sharing the design drawings of his tool for custom fitting bicycles.